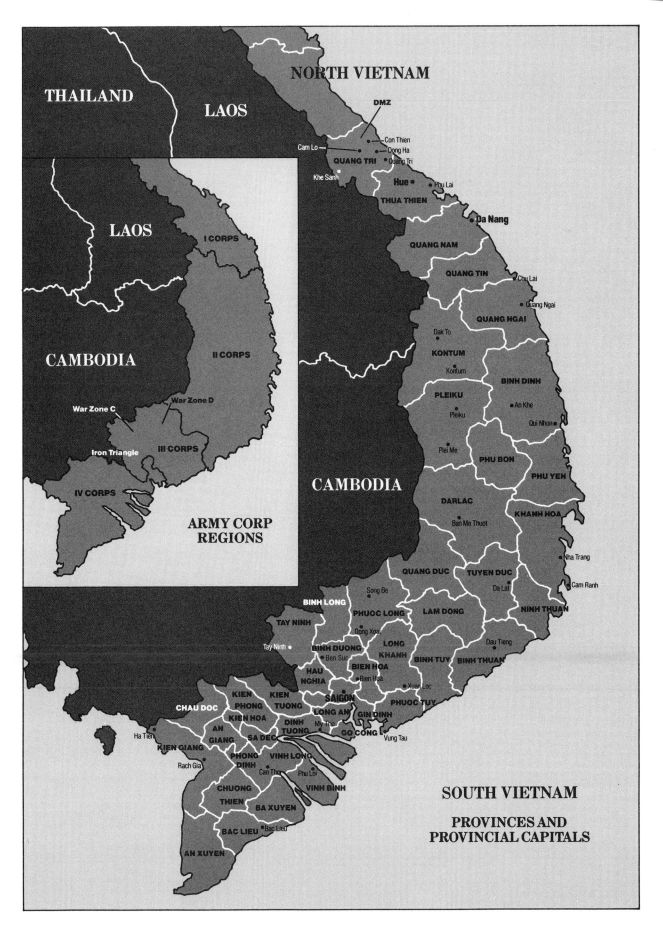

THAILAND

LAOS

NORTH VIETNAM

DMZ

LAOS

CAMBODIA

ARMY CORP REGIONS

I CORPS

II CORPS

War Zone C

War Zone D

Iron Triangle

III CORPS

IV CORPS

Cam Lo — Con Thien
Dong Ha
QUANG TRI Quang Tri

Khe Sanh

Hue • Phu Lai
THUA THIEN

Da Nang

QUANG NAM

QUANG TIN Chu Lai

Quang Ngai

QUANG NGAI

Dak To

KONTUM

Kontum

BINH DINH

PLEIKU An Khe

Pleiku

Qui Nhon

Plei Me

PHU BON

PHU YEN

DARLAC

Ban Me Thuot

KHANH HOA

Nha Trang

QUANG DUC

TUYEN DUC

Da Lat

Cam Ranh

CAMBODIA

BINH LONG

Song Be

NINH THUAN

PHUOC LONG

LAM DONG

TAY NINH

Dong Xoai

BINH DUONG

LONG KHANH

Dau Tieng

BINH TUY

BINH THUAN

Tay Ninh •

Ben Suc

BIEN HOA

HAU NGHIA

Bien Hoa

CHAU DOC

KIEN PHONG

KIEN TUONG

SAIGON

LONG AN

Xuan Loc

PHUOC TUY

KIEN HOA

DINH TUONG

GIN DINH

AN GIANG

SA DEC

My Tho

GO CONG

Ha Tien

KIEN GIANG

Vung Tau

PHONG DINH

VINH LONG

Rach Gia

Can Tho

Phu Loi

CHUONG THIEN

VINH BINH

SOUTH VIETNAM

BA XUYEN

BAC LIEU

Bac Lieu

PROVINCES AND PROVINCIAL CAPITALS

AN XUYEN

THE EYEV
HISTORY
VIETNAM
BY GEORGE ESPER AND

BALLANTINE BOOKS

THE EYEWITNESS HISTORY OF THE VIETNAM WAR 1961-1975

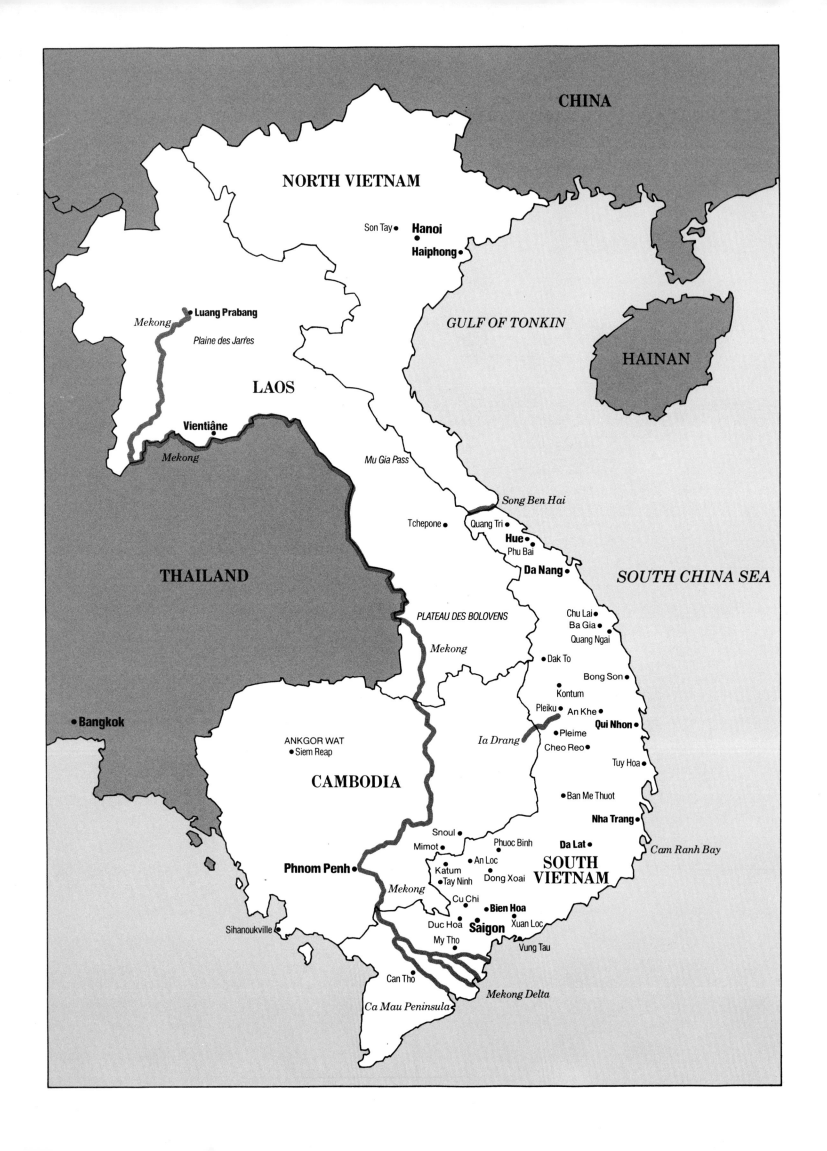

VITNESS
Y OF THE
M WAR 1961-1975
THE ASSOCIATED PRESS

NEW YORK

Editor-in-Chief: Dan Perkes
Author: George Esper
Photo Editor: Carol Deegan
Darkroom Supervisor: Paul J. Shane
Darkroom Technicians: Mauro De-Luca, Richard Del Mastro, Timothy Donnelly, Peter Hermann III, Jesus Medina, Guy Palmiotto, Maurice Pena-herrera, Stan Shapiro, Jim Spiri

Library of Congress Cataloging in Publication Data
Main entry under title:

The Eyewitness history of the Vietnam war.

1. Vietnamese Conflict, 1961–1975. I. Associated Press.
DS557.7.E93 1983   959.704'3 83-45136
ISBN 0-345-30865-4

Manufactured in the United States of America

First Edition: November 1983

10 9 8 7 6 5 4 3 2 1

To those who covered the war in Vietnam,
To those who fought it,
And especially to four Associated Press
photographers who did not return from it,
Bernard Kolenberg, Huynh Thanh My,
Oliver Noonan and Henri Huet,
This book is dedicated.

President and General Manager

CONTENTS

Acknowledgments

Special thanks to my colleagues Hugh Mulligan and Jim Lagier for their good advice, encouragement and other contributions.

A sincere thank you to AP President Keith Fuller, whose continuing faith in me led me to this assignment.

My thanks to Colonels Al Mock and John Grant and the staff of the U.S. Army Military History Institute at Carlisle Barracks, Pennsylvania, for helping me on these long patrols into the past.

My deepest appreciation to everyone around the Boston and New York AP bureaus and the house, who had to put up with me while I was agonizing over these words, particularly Diane, who helped me so much in the organization, Mike and Tom.

I want especially to thank all my colleagues in the Saigon press corps with whom I shared that dramatic decade, particularly Peter Arnett, Bob Tuckman and Ed White.

And finally, a thank you to the many veterans, their families and their friends who lived these years and who graciously and sometimes in sadness contributed their personal letters, photos and remembrances, including Bill Ahearn, Ed Bell, Maggie Burnett, Bob Chadbourne, Colonel King James Coffman, William Davis, Chuck Dean, Brian Delaney, Rick Ducey, Tom Durant, Frank Faulkner, Gerald FitzGerald, Jeanne FitzGerald, Henry and Ida Judge, Paul Kalill, Edith Knox, Michael Kukler, Tom Lareau, Scott Low, Tim Manigan, Charles and Edna McMahon, Mike McPhee, Bill Plude, Michael Shores, Colonel Billy Spangler, Bob and Eileen Sullivan, Colonel Harry Summers, Jr., Lieutenant Colonel (ret.) Val Tully, Marguerite Tussey.

—George Esper
Boston, Massachusetts
July 1983

THE EYEWITNESS HISTORY OF THE VIETNAM WAR 1961-1975

PROLOGUE

December 22, 1961. For 25-year-old Tom Davis the day began like any other since his arrival in Vietnam in May. Scheduled to take his men and electronic equipment into the field to monitor Viet Cong radio broadcasts, he looked forward to another uneventful day. His thoughts on that warm December morning turned, as they often did, to his family—his wife, Gerrie, and his 13-month-old daughter, Cindy. Some 10,000 miles away they were preparing the house for the holidays. This would be the first Christmas he would spend apart from them.

When first assigned to Vietnam, Davis had had to search out the country on a map. Even now, after six months in the rice paddies and jungles with the 3rd Radio Research Unit, the country seemed strangely new and exciting. "It is really an experience for me," he wrote. "The country is really very beautiful and the people fascinating. I believe I have really learned a lot since coming here."

Despite missing his family, Davis felt proud to be serving his country. "You did your share in the 40s," he had written his father, James Clarence "Bum" Davis, who had fought in the Second World War. "Now it's my turn." And, like many of his fellow advisers, he felt certain that his work in Vietnam was important. "I feel a little proud about this deal. I just hope that our little bit will help to ease things in this part of the world. I don't feel too badly about having to be here when I think of all the potential good it will have for this country."

Initially, Davis' brushes with the enemy had been slight. As the months wore on, however, the war seemed to be closing in as communist attacks steadily increased. In August, he wrote to his father telling him of the narrow escape of two U.S. advisers from an enemy ambush:

We became a little more involved in this conflict yesterday.... It looks like the bad guys have gotten the word to start giving us hell. It breaks the daily routine even though it could become a bit dangerous. I didn't really get shaky until I realized that I was very lucky. I had worked the night before and I and another fellow came over the road earlier that morning on our way back to town. So it's just chance that it was Bill instead of us that got hit. Fortunately, nobody was hurt.

Later on December 22, returning from the field in a truck transporting himself and 10 South Vietnamese soldiers along a road 12 miles west of Saigon, the young Tennessean glanced uneasily into the brush lining the roadside. Although the road appeared clear and an ARVN outpost lay less than a mile ahead in the village of Duc Hoa, Davis remained alert. The guerrillas had an uncanny knack for appearing out of nowhere.

Suddenly, an explosion rocked the ¾-ton truck, ripping through the tailgate. A remote-controlled mine planted in the road had been detonated as the truck rolled by. The damaged vehicle limped forward another 30 yards before dying along the right side of the road. Immediately, the VC opened fire, raking the disabled vehicle with submachine gun fire, cutting down the Vietnamese soldiers as they struggled out of the rear of the truck.

Riding in the cab, Davis had escaped the mine explosion. Now he reacted. Snatching up his M-14 carbine, he scrambled from the smoking cab and returned the fire. A VC bullet found its mark, piercing his head and killing him instantly.

Specialist 4 James Thomas Davis, RA 14 696 877, Livingston, Tennessee, had made the ultimate sacrifice for his country—his life. He had also secured for himself a tragic niche in American history: the first American to die in combat in Vietnam. He would not be the last.

JAMES THOMAS DAVIS
TENNESSEE
SP4   US ARMY
JUNE 1 1936   DEC 22 1961
ARCOM

Left: *Specialist 4 James T. Davis.* Top: *Mr. and Mrs. James C. Davis stand beneath a portrait of their son James T. (Tom) Davis and his young daughter, Cindy, in their Livingston, Tennessee, home.*

CHAPTER 1
THE BEGINNING

Two million seven hundred thousand American soldiers served in Vietnam; 57,939 of them, including Tom Davis, lost their lives. Many more came back "walking wounded," emotionally or physically scarred. None who served returned unaffected. Eventually, the war spilled over into America, touching off a wave of riots and social upheaval, and provoking a crisis of national self-doubt and reevaluation that rocked the foundation of American society. Few Americans who lived through the war will forget it.

But how did we get there? How did a young man like Tom Davis from a small town in Tennessee come to lose his life in a Southeast Asian jungle? Why did the United States commit itself to a conflict which would take the lives of nearly 2.5 million Vietnamese, Cambodians, Laotians, French and Americans and cost the United States more than $150 billion in military aid?

America's involvement in Vietnam began during the Second World War. American OSS teams (Office of Strategic Services—the forerunner of the CIA) joined with Vietnamese guerrillas in fighting the Japanese invaders. Leading these guerrillas was a Vietnamese revolutionary named Nguyen Ai Quoc, more widely known as Ho Chi Minh.

Left: *October, 1952. French paratroopers fresh from a defeat at the hands of Viet Minh forces retreat across a stream in the Nghia Lo district of North Vietnam.* Above: *Ho Chi Minh. At his death in 1969, even the South Vietnamese newspaper* Vietnamese Guardian *admitted "with his passing for better and for worse, Vietnam loses its unique politician of truly international status."*

Left: *1945. Ho poses with Vo Nguyen Giap, the Minister of Interior in his short-lived independent Vietnamese government.* Center: *Once again on the run. Ho in North Vietnam in 1949.* Right: *Ho welcomes Russia's recognition of himself and his government, January 31, 1950.*

As the war drew to a close, the Allies turned their attention toward shaping the new world. In Vietnam, this meant, as far as American President Franklin Delano Roosevelt was concerned, preventing the French from reestablishing their colony. Indochina had been "liberated by American aid and American troops," Roosevelt declared, and "should never simply be handed back to the French, to be milked by their imperialists."

As an alternative, Roosevelt offered to turn the country over to the Chinese. However, the Chinese Nationalist leader Chiang Kai-shek vehemently declined the offer. "Under no circumstances," he declared, would he accept. "They are not Chinese. They would not assimilate into the Chinese people." Two thousand years of failed Chinese attempts to conquer and control the Vietnamese had taught him a lesson the French and the United States would not learn for another 30 years.

In April of 1945 Roosevelt died, leaving his plans for Indochina unfulfilled. Meanwhile, in Europe, other events were taking place which would radically alter U.S. Indochina policy. With the Cold War already brewing, the United States sought a European alliance that would include France to offset the Soviet Union's growing influence.

Unwilling to risk a split with France, new President Harry Truman backed down from Roosevelt's hard-line stance on Indochina. Under the new policy, which could be described as a guarded neutrality, the United States chose not to oppose the French occupation. But they insisted that any U.S. military aid sent to France not be used in Vietnam.

By the end of the year all American

His battle with the French over, Ho Chi Minh raises his glass for a toast with Mao Zedong at a reception marking the signing of major aid agreement with China.

French Marine commandos wade ashore off the Annam coast in July, 1950. One of the three ancient kingdoms of Vietnam, Annam encompassed the long, central section of Vietnam stretching from the Red River Delta in the north to the Mekong Delta in the south.

forces had been withdrawn from the country. Despite losing the support of the United States, Ho Chi Minh and his guerrillas continued to work toward their independence. Earlier that year, on September 2, Ho and several thousand Viet Minh troops (along with members of the OSS) had marched into Hanoi and declared the independence of their country. Now, in 1946 with the French maneuvering to reestablish control, Ho moved his troops and political officers into Hanoi and prepared for the inevitable conflict that would follow.

In November, negotiations with the French in Hue and Paris broke down, and soon after, fighting erupted in the northern provinces between the French and Viet Minh troops. In the south, the French established a power base in Saigon while in the north Ho retreated to the mountains, a guerrilla once more. The stage had now been set for the first Indochina war.

For three years the United States maintained its neutrality in Vietnam. However, in 1950, responding to the growing Chinese communist presence in Southeast Asia, the United States shifted from what had become a pro-French neutrality to one of active aid. On February 7, President Truman officially recognized the French-supported Saigon government of Emperor Bao Dai. In June the United States followed its political support with military aid, sending several DC-3 Dakotas

Above: *June 5, 1949. Emperor Bao Dai (left) and the French High Commissioner (right) exchange letters containing a common declaration of the future regime of the country.* Below: *U.S. Air Force technicians service a C-47 at Do Son airstrip, 12 miles southeast of Haiphong in April, 1954.*

to Saigon. One month later, in July, after the outbreak of war in Korea, the first members of the United States Military Assistance and Advisory Group (MAAG) arrived in Saigon. It was the beginning of a buildup of American forces in Vietnam that would eventually reach 550,000 troops at the height of the war in 1968.

The first Indochina war ended on May 8, 1954, with the defeat of the French at Dien Bien Phu in northwestern Vietnam. In a classic military battle lasting 56 days, the Viet Minh led by General Vo Nguyen Giap smashed the French forces and with them France's hopes of regaining its colony. During the siege, President Dwight D. Eisenhower had nearly been persuaded to order American air strikes in support of the French. Unable to secure approval for the operation from the major United States allies, he abandoned the idea even though he felt Indochina was vital to American interests.

Top: *December 2, 1953. A helicopter hovers over a battalion command post at the start of Operation Castor which established the French base at Dien Bien Phu.* Middle: *French and Vietnamese forces patrol north of Dien Bien Phu in February, 1954.* Bottom: *French soldiers at Dien Bien Phu run for cover as communist artillery pounds their positions. Intended as an offensive base situated to lure Giap and the Viet Minh out into the open, Dien Bien Phu backfired on the French, resulting in their worst defeat of the war.* Far right: *French Union paratroopers search a wooded area near Dien Bien Phu.*

Right: *March 18. Napalm bombs burst over communist-occupied trenches surrounding Dien Bien Phu while French defenders look on from their own trenches (foreground). Throughout most of the 56-day siege, supplies and reinforcements could only be brought in by airdrop to the beleaguered base.*

Left: *April 19, 1954. U.S. personnel, still operating in strictly a support capacity in Vietnam, listen to a short briefing session in Haiphong. Below: After the fall of Dien Bien Phu, supporting Laotian troops fall back across the Mekong river into Laos, abandoning strongpoints in northern North Vietnam. Photo is by Robert Capa.*

The Geneva Agreement of 1954 which ended the war divided Indochina into four parts. Laos and Cambodia were again to become separate countries. Vietnam was divided along the 17th parallel with Ho Chi Minh's government ruling in the north and the southern half under control of the Saigon government. A key provision of the agreement called for national elections to be held in 1956 to settle the question of reunification.

In the year following the Geneva Agreement, France and the United States both sought a hand in the emerging government in the South as American and French agents openly vied for political control. The Americans won out when Ngo Dinh Diem, a Catholic and anticommunist leader, ousted the French-supported Bao Dai and became president of the newly formed republic. By 1956, France had withdrawn all of its troops from South Vietnam, and the United States remained as the only foreign power sup-

Opening of cease-fire talks on July 5, 1954 at Trung Gia, 25 miles north of Hanoi. Top: General Van Tien Dung (seated first from left), head of the Viet Minh delegation, relaxes in a staff hut under a portrait of Ho Chi Minh and a Viet Minh flag. Parachutes, which the Viet Minh claim to have taken from Dien Bien Phu, also hang from the walls. Bottom: Dung gives his opening address before the assembled French and Viet Minh delegates.

12

porting the new Diem regime. Neither the United States, which had already poured more than $1 billion in aid into Vietnam, nor Diem wished to see the communists gain control of South Vietnam. Both, therefore, refused to honor the terms of the Geneva Agreement, arguing that neither had signed it (the United States was only a participant in the agreement, not a signatory). Their refusal marked the beginning of the second Indochina war.

Top left: *French tanks depart from Haiphong on May 11, ending 100 years of French colonial rule in the port city.* Top right: *April 14, 1954. Emperor Bao Dai thanks the officers of the Vietnam National Army in Hanoi.* Bottom: *Geneva, July 21, 1954. Last plenary session on Indochina in the Palais des Nations. Left to right (starting second from left) are Vyacheslav M. Molotov, two unidentified Russians, Anthony Eden, Sir Harold Caccie and W. D. Allen.*

13

Top right: *Aged Vietnamese hold banners and flags celebrating the communist victory and welcoming the victorious troops.*
Top left: *Citizens of Hanoi hang flags and fill doorways in anticipation of the Viet Minh troops. Below: October 9, 1954. Waving to the city's populace, joyous Viet Minh troops enjoy* a "parade of victory" through the streets of Hanoi following the French withdrawal. Thousands of Vietnamese civilians crowded the capital's streets waving flags, cheering and throwing flowers to the crowd of soldiers.

Top left: *March 31, 1955. Loyalist soldiers patrol the streets of Saigon during the civil war between Diem's forces and the Hoa Hao and Binh Xuyen forces.* Top right: *June, 1955. Diem reviews a Vietnamese battalion prior to decorating the outfit for its role in the defeat of the Binh Xuyen, the Hoa Hao and* the Cao Dai—*three political/religious groups that sought to overthrow Diem.* Below: *With banners prominently displayed, nearly 40,000 Saigonese crowd the city's market place in a rally showing support for South Vietnam's Premier Ngo Dinh Diem on May 20, 1955.*

For the next three years the war in the south constituted only a small concern for Diem and the United States. Accordingly, the United States maintained a low profile. By 1959, there were still only 300 United States military advisers stationed with MAAG in Vietnam. Their main task was to streamline Diem's military forces and to prepare them for the invasion from the north which they assumed would come. That summer, the communists set out to change that.

On a hot July night six American advisers sat in their mess hall inside an old sawmill in Bien Hoa, 15 miles north of Saigon. Sipping soft drinks, they relaxed while watching a new Jeanne Crain movie, *The Tattered Dress*. One of the viewers, Master Sergeant Chester Ovnand, had just finished writing a letter to his wife in Copper's Cove, Texas. In two months, Ovnand would be celebrating his 45th birthday. Another of the Americans watching the film, Major Dale Buis of Imperial Beach, California, had arrived in Bien

eight-year-old son of the Vietnamese mess cook who had been watching the film through a window lay dead along with two Vietnamese soldiers who had been guarding the building.

For almost 10 minutes the Americans hugged the floor, waiting out the attack as bullets continued to rip through the floor and walls of the building. Almost eyeball to eyeball with the 10 guerrilla attackers, they could see them peering in through the torn screen windows. One terrorist succeeded in forcing his way into the mess hall only to be killed when one of his own homemade bombs exploded.

Finally, for a short moment, there was a lull in the shooting. Seizing their opportunity, the remaining Americans rushed to the main door of the mess hall and escaped into the night. By the time South Vietnamese reinforcements arrived, the guerrillas had slipped away.

Over the next two years the war heated up steadily. In 1961, President Diem sent an urgent request to newly

In 1961, President Kennedy (right) *first dispatched Vice President Johnson* (above) *and then General Maxwell Taylor* (below), *the President's special military adviser, to Vietnam.*

Hoa only two days before. Earlier that evening he had proudly displayed the pictures of his three sons to a fellow officer, Major Jack Hallet of Baton Rouge, Louisiana, who had now joined him in viewing the film.

As the first reel ended, Ovnand stood up and turned on the lights to change reels. Instantly, bullets whizzed through the air from three sides of the building. Ovnand fell almost instantly, fatally wounded. Another bullet cut down Major Buis. Leaping over the prone, bleeding body of Ovnand, Major Hallet flicked off the lights before diving to the floor for cover. Outside, the

elected President Kennedy for more aid. In describing the stepped-up communist offensives, Diem noted that "the level of their attacks is already such that our forces are stretched to their utmost."

"We shall promptly increase our assistance to your defense effort," Kennedy told Diem in his reply. The question still remained as to the size and

nature of that assistance. To help answer that question and to show the United States' continued support for the South Vietnamese government, Kennedy dispatched first Vice President Lyndon Johnson and then special military adviser Maxwell Taylor to Vietnam to review the situation there. Both advised the president to provide assistance both in men and equipment.

In December Kennedy made his decision. Not convinced that remaining in Vietnam was the right choice, but unwilling to pay the price in terms of domestic opposition and loss of face abroad, Kennedy opted to increase the amount of United States aid to Vietnam just enough to maintain the status quo.

On December 11, 1961, the United

States aircraft ferry *Core* docked at Saigon. It carried 33 (C) H-21C helicopters along with their pilots and ground crews. These were the first United States helicopters sent to Vietnam. The two helicopter companies raised the total of U.S. personnel in Vietnam to 1,500. Many more were expected. Eleven days later Tom Davis was dead.

CHAPTER 2
THE ADVISERS

Sergeant Tom Lareau jumped at the chance to serve in Vietnam. A 21-year-old farmer from the small Minnesota town of Zumbrota (population 1,800), he felt a strong attraction to this country so alien to the world he had grown up in. "It was because I was young and romantic," he said. "I'd never heard of the place and I wanted to go overseas. I'd been in Germany already, but I wanted to see the Far East."

The country Lareau found when he landed in February, 1961, was certainly different than any he had seen. As he had hoped, he did indeed find his land of exotic beauty and mystery. He also found frustration, hardship and death.

Lareau served in Vietnam as an adviser, part of MAAG. It was the advisers who drew the unenviable task of shaping the ragtag, under-equipped, ill-led South Vietnamese armed forces into a viable, functioning military outfit, capable of fighting the communist insurgency unaided. Operating first on the provincial and regimental levels and later down to the district and battalion levels, the Americans advised the Vietnamese on everything from battlefield tactics and logistics to communications and intelligence. They also offered assistance in many areas outside the military sphere (in conjunction with other U.S. agencies such as the CIA, the Agency for International Development and the United States Information Agency), including health matters, medicine, finances and agriculture. Along the way they battled language and cultural differences, dysentery, hepatitis, malaria, fungus infections, inept leadership and an unyielding climate. It was a tough job, one which demanded determination, patience, ingenuity and courage.

Among the best known of the advisory groups operating in Vietnam were the U.S. Special Forces, also called the Green Berets. The Green Berets had been advising the Vietnamese since 1957 when members of the 1st Special Forces Group helped to train 58 South Vietnamese at the commando training center in Nha Trang. Three years later, in May of 1960, 30 more Special Forces instructors were dispatched from Fort Bragg to South Vietnam to set up a training program for the South Viet-

A U.S. adviser, clad in bush hat and jungle fatigues, keeps a sharp eye on the shoreline with two members of his Civilian Irregular Defense Group (CIDG) unit while patrolling a river near the Cambodian border.

19

namese army. The Special Forces' presence in South Vietnam was established permanently on September 21, 1961, when the 5th Special Forces Group was activated to assume command of all Green Beret operations in Indochina.

In Vietnam, the Green Berets were best known for their part in the development and training of the Civilian Irregular Defense Groups (CIDG). The CIDGs were composed mostly of Montagnard tribesmen who inhabited remote regions of South Vietnam along the Laotian and Cambodian borders. Generally, these units, of which more than 80 were established between 1961 and 1965, kept tabs on the infiltration routes along the borders.

First developed by the Germans during the First World War, the flame thrower, demonstrated here by a U.S. Army instructor to two South Vietnamese soldiers, was used only occasionally in South Vietnam.

Sergeant Stanley Harold of San Augustine, Texas, instructs a Vietnamese soldier in ambush techniques along the Laotian border. Most of the Special Forces camps were located in isolated border areas to monitor communist movement along their supply routes into South Vietnam.

Two U.S. servicemen demonstrate bayonet techniques to a circle of Vietnamese soldiers. Below: February, 1963. Members of the Dan Ve—self-defense corps—receive training at Tan Hiep training center in the Mekong Delta. By 1963, there were nearly 100,000 members of the self-defense corps.

U.S. Army Sergeant First Class William J. Bowen advises a group of volunteers during an operational training mission in December, 1962. U.S. advisers had the unenviable task of making part-time soldiers out of full-time farmers. Facing page: Vietnamese infantrymen scramble from a H-21c helicopter under the watchful eye of their U.S. adviser, Army Major Elmer J. Gainok.

20

Facing page: *A Montagnard tribesman proudly carries his automatic weapon during training at a Central Highlands village in 1962.* Upper right: *Private First Class Michael G. Boyd, of Wilmington, North Carolina, inspects a mortar with a group of Montagnards who are training at Plei Mrong in the Central Highlands.* Lower top left: *Montagnards take part in training exercises outside of Da Nang. Upon completion of their training they would return to the Central Highlands where they would man U.S. CIDG camps.* Lower middle left: *Montagnards are issued weapons at a U.S. Special Forces camp near Ban Me Thuot.* Lower bottom left: *Rebellious Montagnards stand beside a machine gun placed at the entrance to their head-quarters in the hamlet of Buon Mo Prong.* Lower top right: *At the city of Ban Me Thuot in Darlac Province, a representative of the GVN addresses a group of Montagnards, assuring them that none will be punished if they return to their camps. One week earlier, upset at their treatment at the hands of the South Vietnamese government, the Montagnards had rebelled, killing many of their Vietnamese officers and deserting their posts.* Lower middle right: *A group of Montagnards enjoy a moment's respite outside a training center in the Central Highlands.* Lower bottom right: *An outfit of elite Montagnard rangers prepare for helicopter training at the highland capital of Pleiku.*

The Montagnards presented several special problems for the Special Forces advisers. Ethnically different from the Vietnamese who shunned them, referring to them as "moi," or savages, the Montagnard tribes could never be induced to give more than token support to the South Vietnamese government. Instead, they remained loyal to the Americans who trained them and fought alongside them.

Culturally, they were even further removed from the Americans than the Vietnamese. As Tom Lareau, one of the first to work with them, relates, this led to some wild misconceptions concerning the tribesmen:

When I went up there, there was very little known about the Montagnards, the various groups of them [Lareau worked with the Rhade tribe]. There were rumors going around that some of these were even cannibalistic. The first thought I had was, "I wonder if these people are cannibals?" There had been no information passed back and I was one of the first that came into contact with them. The first meal we had was a stew which I thought was fairly decent. I reached in and I pulled out a hand. It was very humanoid and I thought, "Am I eating baby?" I wasn't. It was monkey, but the thought was there.

Tom Lareau (right), with American and South Vietnamese buddies sharing a meal in An Ninh in 1965.

The people that Lareau met were vastly different from any he and the other advisers had ever come in contact with. Not all the advisers succeeded in establishing a rapport with them. "There had been several people who preceded me who did not seem to get on well with the people and the rea-

son is that they insisted on their American food and American customs and traditions," he observed. "I kind of just sat around for a while and observed what was going on. I found out that, much different from us, they believed in evil spirits in the rocks and trees and certain paths you could walk and certain others you couldn't." Lareau also observed the rigid separation of

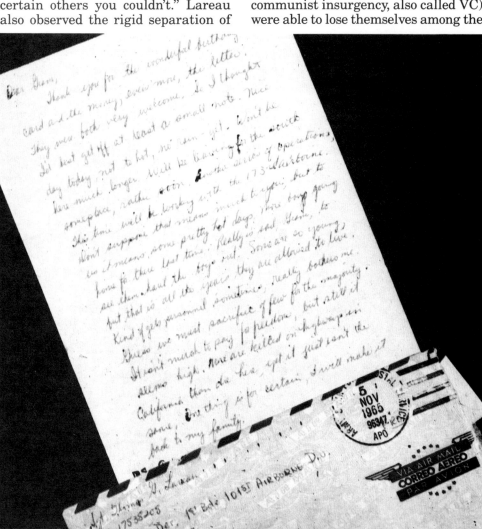

Tom Lareau's letter to his grandmother in Minnesota, November 5, 1975.

Tom Lareau (right) attached to the 101st Airborne in military intelligence in Tuy Hoa in September, 1965.

unmarried men and women, between whom no contact was allowed. As he noted, "this took some getting used to."

Further complicating the advisers' task was the difficulty which they had in identifying the enemy. Supported in many areas by the peasants, the Viet Cong (the southern members of the communist insurgency, also called VC) were able to lose themselves among the

U.S. advisers and South Vietnamese soldiers leap from a U.S. helicopter into a rice paddy in search of a Viet Cong force near the Cambodian border.

A South Vietnamese patrol carrying a 60mm mortar fords a mountain stream in the thick jungle on Darlac Plateau.

Vietnamese and U.S. soldiers battle fire at MAAG compound in Kontum following a VC grenade attack.

people during the day and harass the government troops by night. Even if an adviser suspected a Vietnamese was a guerrilla, he could rarely prove it. For Tom Lareau, this led to several ludicrous situations. On several occasions, he found himself rubbing elbows with different VC during the day in open-air restaurants. "Across the table from you would be the Viet Cong in his black pajamas with his rifle. You would have your uniform on and your rifle with you and you would say, 'Hi, how are you doing?' And he would go his way and you would go your way. And that night you might have an ambush or a firefight."

In addition to the problems which all the advisers working in Vietnam faced, the U.S. soldiers working with the regular South Vietnamese army faced another, ofttimes more difficult obstacle—the advisers had no actual

Specialist 5 Leon B. Talley of Tacoma, Washington, keeps his carbine ready as his helicopter approaches a landing zone near My Qui in the Mekong Delta.

authority over their South Vietnamese counterparts. They could not make battlefield decisions, they could not discipline South Vietnamese troops, and they could not relieve incompetent commanders. This left the advisers at the mercy of the Vietnamese officers.

The South Vietnamese officer corps saw the role of the American adviser as that of calling in air and artillery support and getting war materials and supplies for them. They often sought to bribe advisers with women and other favors in hopes of obtaining a good performance report or in an effort to get the adviser to overlook certain corrupt practices. Frequently, they would tell the Americans what they thought they wanted to hear rather than the truth in order to avoid any sort of embarrass-

U.S. Army Ranger Captain Richard A. Jones (left) accompanies an American-equipped South Vietnamese patrol in the Plain of Reeds near Saigon, November, 1962.

A Viet Cong soldier blows a victory note in this photograph captured in February, 1963.

ment. In all, it made for an often impossible situation for the U.S. advisers.

Captain Ralph Thomas, a 31-year-old adviser from Calloway, Nebraska, thought he was about to die when the South Vietnamese battalion he was with ran into a Viet Cong ambush in the rice paddies of the Mekong Delta. Small-arms fire tore through the lead company, which included a large number of raw recruits.

"I thought I was about to become another statistic when the First and Second Companies broke and ran," Thomas said. "We beat them back to their positions with rifle butts, but finally, there was no holding them."

Thomas escaped unhurt, but the government troops suffered 36 casualties. It was the second time in Thomas' 10 months of duty in Vietnam accompanying the 1st Battalion, 14th Regiment, that it had walked into an ambush. In each case, the troops had ignored the basic rules of military tac-

General Paul D. Harkins, new commander of U.S. military operations in Vietnam, arrives in Saigon on February 21, 1962, followed by General Lionel C. McGarr, chief of MAAG.

Colonel John Paul Vann shown here in 1968 while working as a regional director of U. S. pacification efforts.

tics, failing to properly secure their flanks.

Symbolic of the pathetic state of the South Vietnamese military forces during this period was the battle of Ap Bac in January 1963. Despite a tremendous firepower and troop superiority, the ARVN 7th Division under the direction of Colonel Bui Dinh Dam failed to capture and defeat a much smaller guerrilla outfit. The South Vietnamese lost 68 men and 100 more were wounded. Three Americans were also killed, ten more were wounded, and five CH-21 helicopters were lost. At best, the Vietnamese soldiers performed dismally. Many actually fled the battle. One U.S. adviser, Lieutenant Colonel John Paul Vann of El Paso, Texas, rounded up a ragtag group of cooks and maintenance and communications personnel to head off the escape of some of the VC through an area abandoned by a force of South Vietnamese Civil Guardsmen. Despite coming under heavy fire, he managed to capture 32 prisoners. It was the highlight of the battle for the South Vietnamese.

The problems of the South Vietnamese army began at the top. General Paul D. Harkins, commander of the United States Military Assistance Command (MACV), which took over for MAAG in early 1962, faced many of the same difficulties as his field advisers. "They would say they were doing one thing, and they weren't doing it at all," Harkins complained. "All they had were a lot of good charts. One general had a room filled with charts. I said, 'Well, are you going to get to work on some of these problems?' He hadn't done anything. He wouldn't leave his headquarters. So I said, 'You haven't been out in the field, nobody has seen you since I've been here. I want you to go out and see what's going on.' He wouldn't do it, so I just went to General Ty, chief of the Vietnamese staff, and told him about the guy, and he had him relieved."

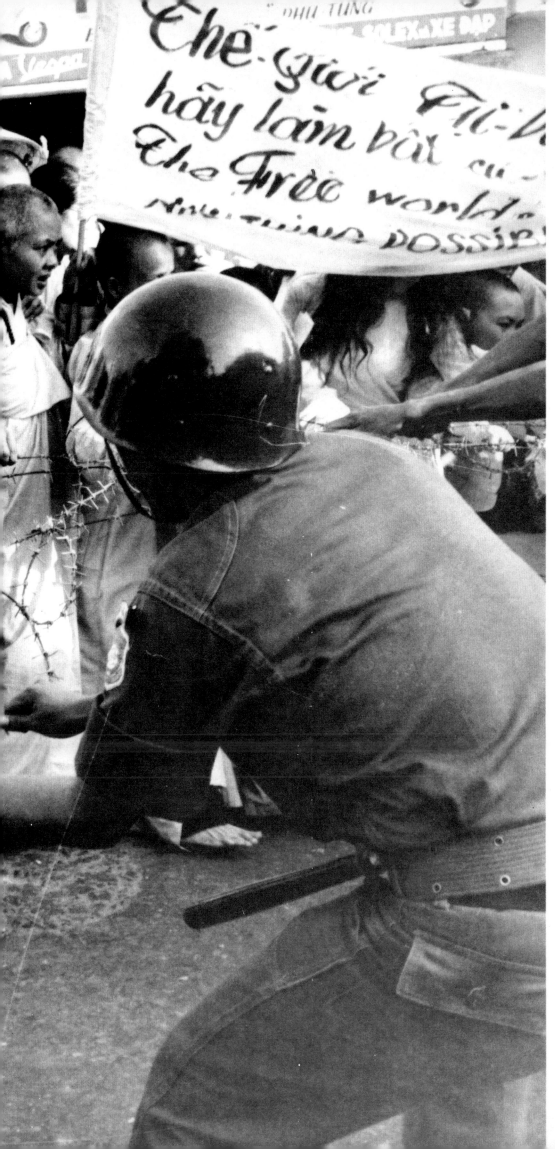

CHAPTER 3
POLITICAL TURMOIL

The morning of June 11, 1963, broke warm and humid. Standing across from a small pagoda off Phan Dinh Phung Street in Saigon, Associated Press correspondent Malcolm Browne was already sweating heavily. Earlier he had received a tip that something special was about to happen here. Glancing about at the growing crowd of Buddhist monks and nuns all chanting the ancient Buddhist prayers in unison, he was sure of it.

The warm, incense-laden air cast a shroud of mystery and foreboding over the scene. Through it all ran a powerful current of pent-up energy, ready to explode. As Browne recalled, "Eyes all around me were fixed straight ahead, almost glazed in the absorption of fervor. But at exactly 9 a.m. it stopped."

Unfurling banners in English and Vietnamese, the 250 Buddhist nuns and bonzes formed into two lines behind a gray sedan. With Saigon police clearing the way, the procession moved slowly through the streets. At Le Van Duyet Street, a major Saigon boulevard, the car rolled to a stop. Quickly, the marchers encircled it. It was now 9:20 a.m.

From the automobile emerged an old Buddhist monk. Accompanied by two other monks, he walked to the center of the circle. There, he seated himself upon a brown pad and closing his eyes, assumed the traditional, cross-legged lotus position. This was the venerable (Thich) Quang Duc. In 15 minutes he would become a saint among Vietnamese Buddhists.

After a moment, one of the monks returned to the center of the circle carrying a clear plastic container brimming with pink gasoline. Lifting it up, he doused the seated monk's head and shoulders, soaking his saffron robes with volatile fluid. After emptying the bottle he placed it beside Quang Duc and returned to the edge of the circle.

Standing less than 20 feet away, Malcolm Browne witnessed the horror that now unfolded.

... I could see Quang Duc move his hands slightly in his lap striking a match. In a flash, he was sitting in the center of a column of flame, which engulfed his entire body. A wail of horror rose from the monks and nuns, many of whom prostrated themselves in the direction of the flames.

From time to time, a light breeze pulled the flames away from Quang Duc's face.

Buddhists tear at barbed wire barricade with bare hands in front of Giac Minh Pagoda in Saigon.

In this sequence of photos, the Vietnamese Buddhist monk 73-year-old Thich (venerable) Quang Duc immolates himself in front of a crowd of Buddhist monks and shocked onlookers. Quang Duc's fiery suicide became a rallying

point for the Buddhist uprising against the Diem government. (Photos by Malcolm Browne, World Press Award, 1964.)

A procession of monks, led by banners proclaiming Quang Duc's sacrifice both in English and Vietnamese, carry the remains of Vietnam's newest saint through the streets of Saigon.

June 19. Buddhist monks carrying pictures of Quang Duc and his suicide and remains conduct a funeral procession through Saigon. His body was later cremated.

Buddhists hold a memorial service for Quang Duc on June 29. Thich Tinh Khiet (center), president of the Buddhist Association in Vietnam, presides over the ceremony at Saigon's Xa Loi Pagoda.

His eyes were closed, but his features were twisted in apparent pain. He remained upright, his hands folded in his lap, for nearly ten minutes as the flesh burned from his head and body. The reek of gasoline smoke and burning flesh hung over the intersection like a pall.

Finally, Quang Duc fell backwards, his blackened legs kicking convulsively for a minute or so. Then he was still, and the flames gradually subsided.

Thich Quang Duc's suicide shocked the world. With one grisly act of protest, the fiery culmination of five weeks of growing unrest, the Buddhists captured the attention of the world and rocked the already shaky administration of President Ngo Dinh Diem. For the Buddhists, this marked the beginning of the end of a regime that had lasted through eight years of war and revolution.

The religious-political crisis started on May 8 when 11 civilians were killed in the old imperial capital of Hue during a demonstration protesting a government ban on the flying of the Buddhist flag at church pagodas. The government said only the national flag could be flown.

Most observers agreed that Diem could have averted the unrest that followed. However, always conscious of the Confucian need to save face, the Vietnamese leader refused to admit his culpability.

As the summer wore on predictions of increased unrest proved eerily prophetic. Following a schizophrenic pattern of repression and conciliation, Diem failed to develop an effective method for handling the situation, and

Xa Loi Pagoda. Vietnamese Buddhists pray before a special altar set up to commemorate Quang Duc. On the altar sits a glass case containing the heart of the dead monk. According to the Buddhists, it did not burn even after five hours of cremation.

all the while the Buddhists' cause gained more and more support. Further dimming any chances for a political settlement were the statements and action of Diem's sister-in-law, Madame Ngo Dinh Nhu, known as the "Dragon Lady," and her husband, Ngo Dinh Nhu. Following Quang Duc's suicide, the impetuous Madame Nhu opined that "all the Buddhists have done for this country is to barbecue a monk."

Powerful, beautiful, arrogant, unpredictable: Madame Nhu.

By the end of June, the Buddhist movement had been taken over by a faction of younger, more politically aware monks led by their enigmatic leader, Thich Tri Quang. These monks had grown up during a politically charged period when war and politi-

With her brother-in-law, Ngo Dinh Diem, looking on, Madame Ngo Dinh Nhu delivers a speech in front of Independence Palace. Below: Madame Nhu observes a group of female cadets on the firing line.

Madame Nhu's husband, Ngo Dinh Nhu, Diem's brother, as historian Joseph Buttinger described him, was a man with "an air of Machiavellian mystery and cynical vanity, wicked intelligence and calculated malice."

cal upheaval were the common state of affairs. Moreover, many such as Thich Tri Quang had fought with the Viet Minh against the French and had developed a keen understanding and appreciation of the power of political agitation and especially the importance of propaganda. These were the tools they were now using to topple the Diem government.

On November 4, Buddhist leader Thich Tri Quang (left) leaves the American embassy where he had sought refuge from Diem following the raid on the pagodas.

Raid on the Pagodas

By late August, an insurmountable impasse had been reached. The doors to the pagodas stood locked and barricaded. Diem, having all but forsaken any attempts at conciliation, had long since retreated to the safety of the imperial palace. Outside, on the streets of the cities, police and soldiers patrolled continuously, keeping careful watch on the pagodas, waiting.

The previous three weeks had witnessed four more Buddhist suicides, three by immolation. Each one stoked the fire a little higher. Each day, Buddhist rallies swelled with new supporters, many of them students and teachers who now joined their cause. Many among the Buddhists felt that the government's fall was imminent. However, Diem's brother Nhu, the chief of Saigon's secret police, had one last gambit to play.

The night of August 20 crackled with tension. Rumors of some sort of move by the government had been running through the city for several days. No one, however, seemed to know what would happen or when. A few minutes after midnight, they found out.

Led by Colonel Le Quang Tung, a fanatical Nhu subordinate, Saigon police along with the colonel's own special force of troops charged the pagodas of

Saigon. Clad in full battle gear, they ripped through the Buddhists' meager defenses, throwing shoulders and rifle butts against the wooden barricades. Overhead, the gongs at the top of the pagodas boomed and clanged wildly, intermingling with the shouts and screams of the Buddhists and soldiers and the occasional crackling of firearms.

For more than two hours the sounds of the raids filled the night. Soldiers systematically combed the pagodas, breaking down doors, statues, shrines and anything else that barred their way. Every monk they found was hauled out and taken away. All over the country, in Hue, Nha Trang and dozens of

July 17, 1963. Police carry a Buddhist demonstrator to a truck in Saigon. The young girl was only one of 200 arrested during the demonstration. Below: A jubilant crowd wheels the head of a statue through the streets of Saigon in a pedicab following the November 1 overthrow of Diem. The crowd later destroyed the head because it bore a resemblance to Madame Nhu.

other cities, hundreds of other pagodas were raided in similar fashion. By early morning, the pagodas lay broken and empty while temporary detention centers swelled with captured and wounded monks.

Although Nhu's raids had temporarily ended the immediate Buddhist threat, the severity of his action had cost him and his brother the support of one essential ally—the United States. As the Buddhist uprising had grown, the Kennedy administration became increasingly disenchanted with Diem. Already they had become disillusioned with the Vietnamese leader's failure to institute much-needed reform and fire corrupt officials. Now, as his

34

public support dissipated rapidly and concern mounted that the political crisis was hurting the war effort, some within the administration voiced the opinion that Diem should be replaced.

In October, a group of 14 dissident Vietnamese generals led by Duong Van "Big" Minh told the United States that they were preparing contingency plans for a coup. They asked how the Americans would respond to a change in government. In Washington, Kennedy received conflicting advice on how to deal with the situation. Some members of the State Department, including the new ambassador, Henry Cabot Lodge, wanted to remove Diem. Others from the Pentagon, especially General Harkins, advised keeping him in power. In the end, the word was passed down quietly to the Vietnamese generals that the United States would not oppose a coup and would support the new regime.

With the United States' imprimatur, the rebels prepared to strike. On November 1, after seizing the police headquarters in Saigon, the rebels attacked the garrison of the palace guard, only five blocks from the presidential mansion, Gia Long Palace. While rebel tanks leveled the garrison, fighter-bombers buzzed the presidential palace, drawing fire from the guards there.

At 4 a.m. on November 2, after spending the night securing control of the city, the rebels opened fire on the presidential palace, pounding the building with cannon and machine gun fire. From the compound, the 150 remaining members of the elite palace guard known as "Diem's Angels" returned the rebel fire in a desperate final stand. Red and yellow tracers streamed across the early-morning skies while flames gutted many of the surrounding buildings.

After two and a half hours of battle, exhausted and suffering from heavy casualties, the palace guards surrendered. They had put up a tough defense against heavy odds. At 6:37 a.m., they raised a white flag from the south wing. Cheers from jubilant rebel soldiers and crowds that had quickly gathered replaced the gunfire.

Sometime during the night, Diem and his brother Nhu slipped away from the palace through a secret tunnel. Eventually they made their way to St. Francis Xavier Roman Catholic Church in the Chinese section of Saigon. Earlier they had tried unsuccessfully to rally commanders from around the country they felt were loyal to them. But now they decided to give up. Diem telephoned one of the coup leaders, and shortly after 9 a.m., several armored personnel carriers and jeeps arrived at the church. Diem and Nhu, their hands tied behind them with

In Honolulu on August 19, retiring Ambassador Frederick E. Nolting (standing) briefs the incoming Ambassador Henry Cabot Lodge (right) on the situation in Vietnam and Southeast Asia.

Rebel troops march through the streets of the capital to break up riots following the coup. Below: Rebel tanks are drawn up in front of the Presidential Palace in Saigon during the coup.

Civilians pass a machine gun to helmeted rebel troops inside the gates of the Presidential Palace. Bottom left: *Rebel troops mill about in front of the palace following the coup on November 3. Although many welcomed Diem's fall, the coup ushered in a period of tremendous political instability.* Bottom right: *March 22, 1964. South Vietnamese Premier, Major General Nguyen Khanh (right) awaits a vote of confidence by the new revolutionary council in Saigon. Sitting at left is Chief of State General Duong Van Minh.*

metal wire, were led into one of the personnel carriers to be taken to the military headquarters in Saigon. They never arrived there. Both were shot to death en route, on orders given by General Minh or General Mai Huu Xuan, an enemy who was one of the first offi-

Delighted Saigon citizens crowd the gates of the Presidential Palace. Bottom left: *Joyful Vietnamese run down La Rue Pasteur in Saigon celebrating the fall of Diem. In the background lies a smoking armored personnel carrier.* Bottom right: *August 16, 1964. After leading the military junta that had toppled Diem, Major General Nguyen Khanh is sworn in as president following an election by the ruling military revolutionary council. Less than a year later, Khanh would be ousted by a group of young officers headed by Nguyen Cao Ky and Nguyen Van Thieu, both of whom had supported Khanh in his rise to power.*

cers to arrive at the church to arrest the brothers. An era had come to an end.

It was 3 a.m. Washington time when President Kennedy was roused from bed by a telephone call from McGeorge Bundy, his special assistant for national security affairs, with the first reports of the fighting that Friday afternoon. (Saigon time is 12 hours ahead of Washington.) The president ordered U.S. military forces from the 7th Fleet, which normally patrolled the South China Sea, toward South Vietnam to protect the 16,500 American troops and the 3,563 civilians in the country.

U.S. officials sought to play down any American connection. State Department Press Officer Richard Phillips told newsmen in Washington that the United States government was in no way involved. In any event, the damage had been done.

The November coup ushered in a period of political instability. Over the next 18 months, the Saigon government would change hands many times. Not until June of 1965 with the ascension of a group headed by General Nguyen Van Thieu and Air Marshal Nguyen Cao Ky would any semblance of stability be reestablished. (Thieu would remain in power for the duration of the war.) However, the cost of that stability was high, for Ky and Thieu's assumption of power signaled the end of any hopes for a civilian-based government in Saigon.

CHAPTER 4
THE TONKIN INCIDENT

When Scott Low of Quincy, Massachusetts, arrived in Vietnam fresh out of college in March 1964, the war was still primarily a Vietnamese affair. The Army briefing booklet given to the 23-year-old lieutenant upon his arrival stressed that he was there only to help the South Vietnamese. Joining the 339th Transportation Company, he did just that, flying up and down the country servicing Army aircraft, recovering downed helicopters and evacuating wounded.

Low marveled at the beauty of the country—"the Riviera of the Orient," as he heard it called—and the warmth of its people. Already, however, he could see the scars of war appearing across the countryside. Soon, defoliation would begin wreaking wholesale destruction upon the land in an attempt to strip the guerrillas of their sanctuaries. "They always pick the prettiest places to fight wars in," he thought.

Still, with fewer than 20,000 troops there, and all of them restricted to advisory roles, the U.S. operation in Vietnam remained on a relatively small scale. The big American bases like Cam Ranh Bay hadn't been built yet. The major battles that would pit American and North Vietnamese infantrymen against each other hadn't yet been fought. Places like Khe Sanh, Ia Drang and A Shau were little more than names on a map.

"It was a different period," Low said. "Cam Ranh Bay . . . was one of the prettiest beaches I've ever seen. There was one Special Forces outpost and a Vietnamese camp there. The rest of it was sand dunes, marshes and no people. I can remember being in the A Shau Valley on a recovery mission when it was a godforsaken place. No one was there except the Viet Cong."

Despite the still limited nature of the U.S. involvement, the conflict itself continued to grow in intensity. More and more, U.S. Special Forces outposts came under attack. More and more, U.S. soldiers were asked to risk their lives in the crucible of battle. On the night of July 6, 1964, at Nam Dong Special Forces camp, one American would prove his mettle many times over.

Vietnamese peasants carry their children to safety as soldiers move in to search a hut in the village of My Son in April, 1964. The war cast its shadow over the lives of more and more Vietnamese as the communists stepped up their war efforts in 1964.

A land of contrasts. Children troop across a dike in the Mekong Delta. Despite its relatively small size (less than 700 miles long and 40 miles wide at its narrowest point), Vietnam contains a wide variety of terrains from the rice paddies and wetlands of the Mekong to the mountainous jungles in the north along the Laotian border.

Above: *Naked Vietnamese youngsters herd water buffalo across a river in the central highlands.* Below: *A baby views the marketplace at Rach Kien in the Mekong Delta from the safety of his bamboo basket.*

Into the Crucible

Located 15 miles from the Laotian border in the northwestern corner of I Corps, the Special Forces camp at Nam Dong had proven untenable. With the camp's defenses in poor condition, the surrounding fields of fire obscured by tall elephant grass, and a shortage of local tribesmen to man the outpost, the Americans decided to transfer the camp over to the local Civil Guard.

In June, the 12-man Special Forces detachment A-726, commanded by Captain Roger H. C. Donlon, arrived at Nam Dong to oversee the transfer. After completing the changeover, Donlon was instructed to open a new camp closer to the Laotian border to keep track of Viet Cong troop movements.

Donlon was a small-town boy from Saugerties, New York. After enrolling as a plebe at West Point, he dropped out and went to work as an airline ticket agent. He said he went into civilian life to find himself. Eventually, however, he found himself back in the Army, returning as an enlisted man and earning his commission at Officer Candidate School. On this night in July 1964, the Army would be glad that he returned.

Walking about the camp, Donlon checked the guards. The day before, an altercation had broken out between the local Nung tribesmen, who had manned the camp for the United States, and the Vietnamese who were assuming control. Donlon suspected that the incident, which resulted in the exchange of several hundred rounds of fire between the two groups, had been instigated by Viet Cong agents, as a prelude to an attack. He was therefore taking extra defensive precautions.

At 2:30 a.m. the attack began. As Donlon moved across the camp, the mess hall in front of him exploded in a white blast. Immediately, mortar rounds burst all over the compound. Inside the radio shack, Sergeant John Houston, 22, of Winter Park, Florida, the youngest member of Donlon's team, scrambled from his bed as the first blasts rocked the camp. Reaching for his radio equipment, he tapped out a hasty message of warning to the B detachment in Da Nang, 30 miles to the east: "Under intense mortar attack..." Before he could complete the message a white phosphorous mortar round landed directly on the radio shack, destroying the building and killing Houston.

Other buildings, including the dispensary and the barracks, also burst into flames as dozens of mortar shells slammed one after another into the mountain camp. Many were killed inside the barracks before they could fire a shot. In the first 15 minutes of the

January 27, 1964. General Harkins greets his new deputy, Lieutenant General William Westmoreland. Called by his classmates at West Point the "inevitable general," Westmoreland took over from Harkins in June.

attack, one-third of the camp's defenders were either wounded or killed.

Outside the camp under the cover of the mortar attack, 500 Viet Cong crept through the tall saw grass to the barbed wire. Cutting through the wire, they tossed hand grenades into a nearby mortar position and then launched two assaults against their inner defenses. The government forces turned their mortars and 57mm guns on them point-blank. With the battle raging about them, nurses crawled along the ground stripping the dead of first aid kits needed for the living.

Donlon raced through a barrage of

A South Vietnamese ranger punishes a farmer with the end of his dagger for allegedly providing government troops with false information on the VC.

rifle fire and exploding hand grenades to cut off the Viet Cong at the main gate. There he killed three members of a commando demolition team. With the gates secured, he then dashed to the mortar emplacement to help his wounded team members. Though bleeding profusely from wounds in his stomach and shoulder, Donlon continued to direct fire against the communist attackers.

As the Viet Cong were about to overrun the east sector, he ran through the camp retrieving weapons and ammunition, receiving a third wound in his leg. Unable to walk, he managed to crawl along the ground, dragging heavy ammunition behind him for 200 yards to another mortar position, where again he directed fire against the Viet Cong who had broken into the inner perimeter of the camp itself.

At dawn, the Viet Cong, without the cover of darkness to mask them, pulled back, carrying their wounded with them. Their withdrawal came just in time, for the defenders at Nam Dong had little ammunition left.

Both sides suffered heavy casualties. Sixty of the camp's defenders, including two Americans, Houston and Master Sergeant Gabriel Alamo, 45, of Lyndhurst, New Jersey, were killed, and 65 were wounded, including four other Americans. The defenders had also killed more than 60 Viet Cong. For his actions in helping to save the camp, Donlon was awarded the Medal of Honor. He was the first U.S. soldier in Vietnam to be so honored.

By August 1964, nearly 300 Americans had died in Vietnam and 1,000 had been wounded. One of the casualties, Captain James Spruill, 33, of Plymouth, North Carolina, had written his wife, Barbara, before he was killed that America should not give up hope.

"We must stand strong and give heart to an embattled and confused people. This cannot be done if America loses heart," he wrote. "Above all, this is a war of mind and spirit. For us to despair would be a great victory for the enemy. At the moment, my heart is big enough to sustain those around me. Please don't let them back where you are sell me down the river with talk of despair and defeat. There is no backing out of Vietnam, for it will follow us everywhere we go. We have drawn the line here, and the America we all know and love best is not one to back away."

America was not about to disengage, for events were to take place in the Tonkin Gulf off the coast of North Vietnam that would plunge the United States deeper into the war and give President Johnson the congressional backing for an all-out escalation in 1965.

The U.S. Navy destroyer Maddox. *The* Maddox *was engaged on an electronic spy mission code-named Desoto when North Vietnamese PT boats attacked the U.S. ship.*

The Tonkin Gulf Incident

On a sunny Sunday afternoon, August 2, 1964, many of the crewmen aboard the U.S.S. *Maddox* were topside sunbathing as the destroyer moved through the Tonkin Gulf, electronically plotting North Vietnamese radar positions as part of a secret spy mission code-named Desoto. The destroyer was 15 miles off the coast of North Vietnam, in international waters. Five torpedo boats, presumably North Vietnamese, could be seen in the distance.

A special communications group picked up some intelligence that the *Maddox* might come under attack. The PT boats showed up as a pinpoint of light in a round, glowing green field in the destroyer's radar room. Radarmen were ordered to keep a close watch on the scope.

The *Maddox* and the torpedo boats had been running parallel to the coast, separated by about 20 miles. The destroyer made a 90-degree turn to see what the torpedo boats would do. They turned to follow. Quietly, word was passed to man battle stations.

Aboard the *Maddox*, Captain John J. Herrick, the commodore in charge of Destroyer Division 192, now gave the go-ahead to fire warning shots if the PT boats got within 5.6 miles. One gun in each of three two-gun mounts fired a five-inch shell at the North Vietnamese boats. Apparently disregarding the warning, the torpedo boats continued to close at high speed.

Lieutenant Raymond Connell, the weapons officer, now started all six guns firing five-inch shells as quickly as they could. The torpedo boats fanned out and fired toward the *Maddox*'s bow, midships and aft. Gordon Cadmus, a quartermaster second class, who was at the helm, grabbed the thick, solid brass wheel and swung the *Maddox* around. The "stingers" (torpedos) passed 100 to 200 yards astern without causing any damage. One of the North Viet-

Soviet-made PT boat similar to that encountered by the Maddox *in the Tonkin Gulf. Eighty-three feet in length and 20 feet across the beam, the boats carried a complement of 17 men and could reach speeds of 40 knots.*

namese boats lay dead in the water, smashed by a direct hit from the *Maddox*. Unable to run, the PT boat continued to fight, dropping another torpedo from its tube.

The lead PT boat aimed again for the *Maddox*'s bow, and the destroyer shifted its fire to counter it. The lead boat and the two accompanying it then dropped astern, firing machine gun bursts at the *Maddox* as they passed under the stern. One round landed a yard below Lieutenant Keith Bane, who was directing the guns at the rear of the destroyer, madly ricocheting around a powder magazine under Bane. Miraculously, it failed to set off an explosion.

The *Maddox* doubled back to try to destroy the PT boats once and for all. At that moment, three jet fighter-bombers from the carrier *Ticonderoga* arrived to help. By now, three torpedo boats either had been hit or were throwing up a smoke screen to throw the *Maddox* off. As the destroyer closed for the kill, one of the jet pilots reported damage to his aircraft and expressed his fear that he might have to ditch his plane. Commander Herbert Ogier turned and followed the disabled aircraft for 20 minutes until the pilot informed him that he would make it. Before he could resume the chase, Ogier was ordered to break off the engagement.

"If they had just turned and run away after we'd started firing at them, then we could have been in trouble," said the skipper Ogier. "They could have said, 'Here we were in international waters, too, and you went and fired at us.' But they came on in and fired torpedoes at us, which was good."

When reports of the *Maddox* reached Washington, President Johnson called for reinforcements. The carrier *Constellation* sped to the scene. So did the destroyer *C. Turner Joy*, whose crew had been scheduled for liberty in Hong Kong.

By Tuesday night, two days after the *Maddox* encounter, the two destroyers maneuvered in the Tonkin Gulf with the *Turner Joy* 1,000 yards astern. The crews, in flak jackets and helmets, were at battle stations from dawn to dusk. The *Turner Joy* was on condition 2, meaning half her crew was at battle stations. Many of the off-duty crewmen were watching a movie, whose last reel was suddenly interrupted.

On the bridge, Ensign John Leeman, who had taken the watch at 8 p.m., reported radar contact. "I saw, with my own eyes, five or more high-speed contacts approaching on the surface-search radar," he said. "I saw this."

The destroyers were about 65 miles from shore. Jets from the carriers

A picture taken from the Maddox *shows one of the attacking PT boats running across the bow of the U.S. destroyer during the August 2 confrontation.*

NORTH VIETNAM

CHINA

Hanoi •
Hon Gai •
Haiphong •

Nam Dinh •

Thanh Hoa •

GULF OF TONKIN

HAINAN

Hon Me •

Hon Ngu •
Vinh •

Vinh Son •
Ron •
Quang Khe •
Dong Hoi •

LAOS

Hue •

THAILAND

Da Nang •

SOUTH VIETNAM

Senator J. William Fulbright. Although the powerful senator from Arkansas heartily supported the Tonkin Gulf Resolution, he soon became an ardent opponent of U.S. policy in Vietnam.

U.S. destroyer Turner Joy *steams across the Pacific. The* Turner Joy *joined the* Maddox *on its patrols on August 3.*

Ticonderoga and *Constellation* streaked to their support. When the radar blips indicated a target at 4,000 yards, Barnhart ordered the *Turner Joy* to open fire. The *Maddox*'s radar did not show anything.

"I had nothing to shoot at," said Connell, the *Maddox*'s weapons officer. "I recall we were hopping around up there, trying to figure out what they were shooting at because we didn't have any targets. We fired a lot of rounds, but it was strictly a defensive tactic. We called aircraft and aircraft was there by this time and they couldn't find anything to shoot at."

Commander Wesley McDonald, guided by the *Turner Joy*'s radar, flew his jet in low several times looking for targets. "I honestly could not see any ships on the surface," said McDonald. The impenetrable darkness nearly led to tragedy as the *Maddox* and the jets almost mistakenly fired upon each other.

David Mallow, a sonarman, who had been roused from sleep to monitor the *Maddox*'s sonar scope, reported hearing and seeing hydrophone noises that

A crewman plots the course of an unidentified plane in the radar room of the U.S.S. Ticonderoga. *Planes from the carrier* Ticonderoga *and the U.S.S.* Constellation *quickly moved to assist the* Maddox *and the U.S.S.* Turner Joy *during the second run on the North Vietnamese PT boats on the night of August 4.*

indicate a torpedo in the water. There were no similar noises detected on the *Turner Joy*, but Lieutenant (j.g.) John Barry III, a gunner specialist who was in the highest manned point on the ship, said he spotted on radar what he presumed to be a boat closing.

"The *Maddox* at that point reported a torpedo in the water," Barry said. "The contact was approximately four thousand yards out on our port quarter, possibly even closer. At this point, we initiated a turn so both the *Turner Joy* and the *Maddox* turned. Then I personally spotted the torpedo."

Seaman Larry Litton, standing next to Barry, said he, too, saw the torpedo at a distance of 50 to 60 yards.

On the *Maddox*, Mallow made 20 or more reports of torpedoes as the destroyer maneuvered in violent, evasive actions.

"They passed the word every couple of minutes to brace yourself, torpedoes coming," said Felix Nerio, a gun pointer in the mount. "I kept grabbing the gun. I grabbed it so hard the stone flew out of my ring." Finally, after two and a half nerve-racking hours, the radar engagement was considered over.

This small naval engagement in which there were no American casualties left many unanswered questions. Hanoi charged that the *Maddox* participated in or provided cover for raids by South Vietnamese PT boats on North Vietnamese islands, a series of operations code-named 34-A. Admiral Thomas Moorer, the Pacific Fleet commander, ordered the *Maddox* and the *Turner Joy* to patrol 50 to 60 miles north of the South Vietnamese PT boat operations. He said this would eliminate American interference and possibly draw the North Vietnamese patrol boats away from the area of the South Vietnamese raids.

After a preliminary review of the August 4 engagement, Captain Herrick cabled Washington:

"Review of action makes many reported contacts and torpedoes fired appear doubtful. Freak weather effects and overeager sonarman may have accounted for many reports. No actual visual sightings by *Maddox*. Suggest complete evaluation before any further action."

Herrick sent a second cable a short time later:

"*Turner Joy* also reports no actual visual sightings or wake. Entire action leaves many doubts except for apparent ambush attempt at beginning. Suggest thorough reconnaissance by aircraft at daylight."

Word of the latest engagement reached Washington shortly before noon just as the National Security Council was about to sit down for a previously scheduled meeting with President Johnson. The White House buzzed with activity as official black limousines pulled up and discharged grim-looking passengers. Sixteen congressional leaders were summoned to the White House and told by the president what he planned to do.

At 11:37 p.m., on August 4, President Johnson went on national television to address the people:

"Repeated acts of violence against the armed forces of the United States must be met not only with alert defenses, but with positive reply."

As he spoke, fighter-bombers pounded PT boat bases and oil depots along the North Vietnamese coast in 64 strikes conducted over a five-hour period beginning at noon Saigon time.

North Vietnamese gunners shot down two American planes and damaged two others. One American pilot, Lieutenant (j.g.) Richard Sather, 26, of Pomona, California, was killed. Another, Lieutenant (j.g.) Everett Alvarez, of San Jose, California, was captured.

Despite the nebulousness of the reports of the Tonkin engagements, President Johnson had successfully used

Above: *President Johnson meets with the National Security Council on August 4 to discuss the Gulf of Tonkin incident. Clockwise from left: USIA director Carl Rowan; Presidential Assistant McGeorge Bundy; Treasury Secretary Douglas Dillon; Emergency Planning director Edward McDermott; Attorney General Robert Kennedy; CIA director John McCone; Undersecretary of State George Ball; Secretary of State Dean Rusk; President Johnson; Defense Secretary McNamara.*

Johnson hits the campaign trail on September 7 at a Labor Day rally in Detroit. Below: Senator Ernest Greuning of Alaska (left) chats with Senator Wayne Morse (right) of Oregon. Greuning and Morse cast the only dissenting votes to the Tonkin Resolution.

Above, below, and below right: *U.S. Army soldiers survey the wreckage of a B-57 bomber on November 1 at Bien Hoa air base, the results of a VC mortar attack the previous night.*

the incident as justification to launch air strikes against North Vietnam and to gain from Congress the Tonkin Gulf Resolution, congressional authority "to take all necessary measures to repel any armed attack against the forces of the United States and to prevent further aggression."

The year of 1964, the Year of the Dragon in the lunar new year of the calendar, ended with stepped-up attacks by the Viet Cong. In November, Viet Cong gunners hit Bien Hoa Air Base north of Saigon with mortars, killing five Americans and wounding 76. On Christmas eve, terrorists bombed a Saigon hotel where American officers were staying, killing two and wounding 98.

The Tonkin incident had changed the face of the war and set the stage for the massive American buildup that would follow.

Above: *The mortar attack on the Bien Hoa airfield also destroyed part of the barracks for the 318th U.S. Army Aviation Company.*

CHAPTER 5
THE BUILDUP

1965 began peacefully. As the Vietnamese celebrated the lunar New Year festival of Tet, the war paused. The Viet Cong even allowed government troops to pass unmolested on their way home for the holiday. All across Vietnam, glasses of rice brandy were raised in toasts. People feasted on "banh chung" (rice pudding), chanted prayers for the dead soldiers and sought the advice of astrologers about the future.

On the night of February 6, Jesse Pyle stood guard duty outside the U.S. military compound near Pleiku. A city of 100,000, Pleiku housed the headquarters of II Corps, the military region stretching across the center of South Vietnam from the coastal plains westward to the highlands.

At 12:00 midnight, the ceasefire ended, and in the early hours of the morning of February 7, the 35-year-old sergeant from Springfield, Oregon, looked forward to several more hours of uneventful watching.

Then Pyle saw them. In the grass and underbrush surrounding the camp, shadows shifted and moved, heading toward the barbed wire like a disjointed wave. The Korean War veteran did not have to be told what the shadows were. Firing blindly across the perimeter, Pyle alerted the rest of the 400 Americans in the camp before he was cut down by a bombardment of grenades. Mortars followed, jarring the barracks windows and sending shell fragments across the compound. Rudely awakened by the blast, the Americans leapt to return fire through the windows and from behind walls.

One hundred Viet Cong troops struck simultaneously at Camp Holloway airstrip four miles away. Sappers broke through the outer defenses and moved along rows of parked helicopters and light planes, setting off explosive charges.

In the scant 15 minutes that they lasted, the battles took a heavy toll. Eight Americans were killed and 126 were wounded. Also, more than 20 aircraft were destroyed or damaged.

As the battlefield report was flashed back to Saigon, General William C. Westmoreland, the new commander of the 23,500 American military men now in Vietnam, met with Ambassador Maxwell Taylor and McGeorge Bundy,

November 8, 1965. U.S. paratroopers from the 173rd Airborne Division squat in tall elephant grass in War Zone D north of Saigon looking in the direction of nearby sniper fire.

49

Pedestrians, cars and pedicabs fill the streets of Saigon in April, 1965. Below right: *U.S. aircraft carrier* Hancock. *The* Hancock *and its complement of 75 planes participated in the February 7 raid on North Vietnam along with the carriers* Coral Sea *and* Ranger.

an aide to President Johnson who was on a fact-finding mission. They recommended prompt retaliation.

By 2:38 p.m., Saturday, February 6, Washington time, President Johnson had assessed the war reports. After consultations with Secretary of Defense Robert McNamara, who was home with pneumonia; acting Secretary of State George Ball; and General Earle Wheeler, Chairman of the Joint Chiefs of Staff, Johnson convened a meeting of the National Security Council at 7:45 p.m.

"I've had enough of this," President Johnson told the council. "I want three things. I want a joint attack. I want it to be prompt. I want it to be appropriate."

Within four hours of Johnson's order,

Presidential aide McGeorge Bundy (front) arrives in Saigon on February 4 on a three day fact-finding tour of South Vietnam. Behind Bundy is U.S. Ambassador Maxwell Taylor.

Above: *A U.S. A-4 Skyhawk releases a 2,000-pound bomb on a VC target in South Vietnam in November, 1965.* Below: *Aerial photo of Vinh Linh in North Vietnam following a U.S. bombing strike in February, 1965.*

at 2:00 p.m. Saigon time, Sunday, February 7, U.S. jet fighter-bombers catapulted from the carriers *Coral Sea,* *Hancock* and *Ranger* in an aerial offensive code-named Flaming Dart. Unaccompanied by any South Vietnamese planes, which had been grounded by poor weather conditions, 49 Navy A-4 Skyhawks and F-8 Crusaders streaked over North Vietnam, broke through the heavy cloud cover, and demolished a guerrilla staging area at Dong Hai, 40 miles north of the demilitarized zone.

The attack, Flaming Dart I, marked the official start of the American air war against North Vietnam. It also signaled yet another escalation of the conflict, contrary to official statements from Washington that the United States did not want to expand the war.

"I think it's quite clear that this was a test of will, a clear challenge of the political purpose of both the United States and South Vietnamese governments," said McNamara. "It was a test and a challenge, therefore, which we couldn't fail to respond to... without misleading the North Vietnamese as to our intent and the strength of our purpose to carry out that intent."

President Johnson declared: "As the United States government has frequently stated, we seek no wider war. Whether or not this course can be maintained lies with the North Vietnamese aggressors."

Just the same, President Johnson ordered a Marine battalion equipped with Hawk surface-to-air missiles into Da Nang to protect the air base. Simul-

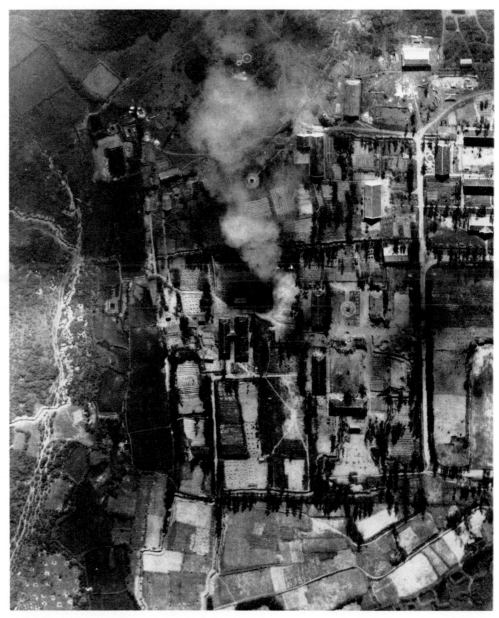

51

taneously, he ordered nearly 2,000 wives and children of American personnel home. The first group flew out of Saigon on February 9.

"We have no choice but to clear the decks," said Johnson.

The Viet Cong were not idle either. Three days later they retaliated.

Specialist 5 Ernest Schultz III, a 24-year-old helicopter crewman from Fort Myers, Florida, viewed the escalation of the war with growing uneasiness. Stationed in the coastal city of Qui Nhon with the 140th Maintenance Detachment, he had watched the conflict grow day by day. In February, he shared his fears with his German wife, Brigitte. For the first time, he recognized the possibility that he might be killed.

"The VC have really been raising hell around here," he wrote. "Never before have I really worried about not coming home to you alive, but now I'm sort of worried."

Rescuers dig through the wreckage of the Viet Cuong Hotel in the coastal city of Qui Nhon for survivors of the terrorist bombing.

"Each night," he continued, "you can hear a battle going on. And the VC north of here are moving down toward us more and more. If you hear anybody say that Americans don't fight over here, tell them they're crazy. There were about 20 Viet Cong shooting at our chopper today not very far from here."

Another American who lived with Schultz in the Viet Cuong Hotel in Qui Nhon, Specialist 5 Robert Marshall, 21, of Premier, West Virginia, assured his wife, Sara, in letters that he was all right and everything was okay. She worried every time she heard or read about the fighting in Vietnam. Mar-

shall had only 23 days left to serve of his 12-month tour. Then he would be on his way home for a reunion with Sara and would hold his 3-month-old daughter, Michelle May, for the first time. He and Sara counted each day.

On the night of February 10, Marshall was lying on his bed reading a C.S. Forester adventure novel by the light of a street lamp that shone through his window on the third floor. Since the end of Tet, lights had been turned off at 6:00 p.m. as a precaution.

At about 8:00 p.m. rifle fire in the street below shook Marshall back to reality.

Marshall grabbed his rifle, rushed to the balcony outside his window, and emptied his weapon into the Viet Cong, killing two of them. As he raced back to his room for more ammunition, three strategically placed explosive charges ripped through the 27-room hotel, tumbling its four stories like a house of cards and burying Marshall, Schultz

and many other Americans under a pile of rubble.

"It just completely disintegrated," Marshall said. He saved his life by tossing his steel folding cot on top of himself to cushion himself from the debris. For nearly three hours he struggled to dig himself out, talking occasionally to three other Americans buried nearby beyond his reach.

Schultz was not as lucky. He was among 23 U.S. servicemen who died, the largest number of Americans killed to date in a single attack. Two days later, his wife Brigitte would receive his letter saying he was worried about not making it back to her.

Another soldier, Abe Abendschein, 30, of Deptford, New Jersey, was trapped for 35 hours in a splintered cavern measuring about six feet by two feet by two feet. Concrete was piled 15 feet above him and to a greater distance on each side. He called out for help. The cries of another young man whose leg was being amputated drowned him out.

Engineers pulled out some of the entombed from a tunnel hand-drilled into the floor above. Abendschein hung on for dear life even though he was reeling from a three-inch gash in his head and the sweltering 90-degree heat. After all, he had only 20 days left to serve in Vietnam. Finally, voice contact was established with Abendschein.

"Are you all right?" asked Warrant Officer Eugene Lowe.

"Sure, I'm all right. Is this town on-limits tonight?"

Specialist 5 Pedreno Ebos, a Hawaiian soldier, volunteered to work his way down through the debris when rescuers ran into trouble. Ebos triggered a small landslide that poured debris on Abendschein's back.

"Get the hell out of here and leave me," Abendschein yelled. "Don't get caught. Send me down a hammer and chisel and I'll dig my own way out."

The rescuers sent down the tool and Abendschein began chopping away at the concrete. At the other end, three feet away, Ebos and other rescuers finally broke through, just as Abendschein did. But the holes were at different places and neither was wide enough alone for Abendschein to escape. Abendschein laughed even though he would be stuck in his tomb through the night.

To boost his morale, he was told of retaliatory air strikes. Nearly 200 American and South Vietnamese warplanes attacked barracks and supply depots inside North Vietnam in Operation Flaming Dart II, the biggest aerial offensive yet.

As dawn first approached, low-flying jets and South Vietnamese mortar fire in the region reverberated through the area, sliding the debris farther. An American officer woke the exhausted Abendschein up by pouring a cup of coffee into his face. Exhaustion was also taking hold of the rescuers. Two fresh Montagnard tribesmen from a Special Forces company guarding the wreckage took over. They began digging at 5:40 a.m. Two hours later, Abendschein surfaced with a big grin on his face.

Now the Americans would come in force. As battlefield losses mounted for the Saigon forces and the air war escalated, President Johnson approved sending the first U.S. Marine combat units to South Vietnam. Officials said

Members of the 9th U.S. Marine Expeditonary Force (the name was later changed to Marine Amphibious Force) scramble ashore onto the beach at Da Nang on March 8.

Above: *August 14. 2,800 men of the 7th Regiment, 1st Marine Division, trudge through the sand at Chu Lai to establish a beachhead.* Below: *Once on the beach at Da Nang, Marines take up defensive positions.*

their role would be to beef up the defenses of Da Nang Air Base and free South Vietnamese troops serving as security forces to maneuver in the field and pursue the Viet Cong. By now, the United States had launched Operation Rolling Thunder, a series of sustained air strikes over North Vietnam.

...To the Shores of Da Nang

March 8. Rough seas in Da Nang Bay tossed the landing craft around as the first troops of the 4,000-man 9th Marine Expeditionary Brigade prepared to shove off. At 9:00 a.m., the operation, code-named Red Beach Two, began under gray skies.

As the enclosed landing craft headed the half-mile toward the beach from the 7th Fleet transport ships, the rough seas almost engulfed them.

At 9:03 a.m., the Marines landed. The first Marine ashore was Gary Parsons of Springfield, Illinois, a squad leader. Within minutes, several hundred Marines, in field helmets and full combat packs, took up defensive positions along the length of Nam O Beach, 10 miles west of Da Nang. Later that afternoon U.S. C-130 transports would land at Da Nang carrying the rest of the brigade, the 1st Battalion of the 9th Marine Regiment from Okinawa.

As the Marines charged onto the beach, their weapons ready, they were welcomed by groups of Vietnamese girls clad in the traditional "ao dai"s (silk tunics over pants). As the soldiers approached, the young girls hung leis of red gladiolas and yellow dahlias around their necks. Behind them, an

A garland of leis hanging around his neck, Brigadier General Frederick Karch, commander of the 9th Marine Expeditionary Brigade, watches the landing with South Vietnamese General Nguyen Chanh Thi, IV Corps commander. Thi was later ousted from his post during a bitter political struggle with Air Marshal Nguyen Cao Ky.

official Vietnamese welcoming committee including the mayor of Da Nang and General Nguyen Chanh Thi waited to extend their greetings along with U.S. Marine Brigadier General Frederick Karch, the commander of the brigade.

For some of the Marines, it was already their second tour of duty in Vietnam. Many of them, like Lieutenant Murphy McCloy, 25, were glad to be back. As he explained, "I feel that, if my country is to be engaged out here, I would like to be a small part of it." All too soon for some, they would become too much a "part of it."

Attack on the Embassy

Shortly before 11:00 a.m. on March 30, a black Citroen sedan turned in the street next to the U.S. Embassy, a five-story concrete building. As the sedan stopped, a Saigon police officer told the driver to move on. The driver said he had engine trouble. Suddenly, a motorcycle pulled up and whisked away the driver. The policeman, sensing something was amiss, fired, wounding the cyclist, who fell to the street. At that moment, the policeman's world exploded.

Two hundred and fifty pounds of explosives planted in the stalled sedan detonated, ripping a gaping hole in the side of the embassy and spraying the people inside with shards of glass from the windows.

One block away, Captain Don Elledge of Mabank, Texas, saw a flash and then heard the tremendous boom. Looking toward the embassy, he saw a scene of great destruction. "Every window in the embassy appeared to have been smashed," Elledge said. "Even the windows in the back of the embassy were broken, and the walls were sagging."

The blast flattened Sergeant Lyle Goodwin, of Pekin, Illinois, who was 50 yards across the street.

"I looked up from the street and saw a plume of flames and smoke rising to about thirty feet," Goodwin said. "As I ran across the embassy, I fell over two policemen who had been killed. Then I met a Vietnamese soldier and we concentrated on the Vietnamese homes opposite the embassy that had been smashed. I helped an old Vietnamese

Spattered with blood from a head wound caused by flying glass, Deputy Ambassador U. Alexis Johnson is led from the U.S. Embassy following the terrorist bombing.

Pandemonium reigns in front of the U.S. Embassy as a U.S. Air Force non-com tends to wounded Vietnamese woman.

lady who had been injured in the leg from her house. Then I went up to the embassy to see what I could do."

Manolito Castillo, a 26-year-old Filipino serving in the U.S. Navy, died in the doorway of the embassy. Barbara Robbins, a 21-year-old embassy secretary from Denver, was killed at her desk. She had just written home about her "fascinating job in a fascinating place."

In all, 20 Vietnamese were killed and 130 were wounded, many of them just passing by or in a restaurant that was destroyed across the street. Fifty-two Americans, including Deputy Ambassador U. Alexis Johnson, were wounded in addition to two killed.

President Johnson learned of the terrorist attack during a formal dinner for the visiting president of Upper Volta. He reacted with bitterness.

"Outrages like this," he said, "will only reinforce the determination of the American people and the government to continue and to strengthen their assistance and support for the people and government of Vietnam."

The president did exactly that. In the

The wreckage of the consulate section of the embassy. Flying glass accounted for many of the injuries, including the blinding of two Navy officers.

spring, the first Army combat units and the 3rd Marine Division arrived. American troop strength tripled between January and June of 1965, to 75,000 troops.

On June 9, the White House disclosed that General Westmoreland had the authority to send American troops into combat "when other effective reserves are not available and when in his judgment the general military situation urgently requires it."

Now for the first time, the United States could go beyond its advisory role and pursue the enemy.

Dead and wounded are carried from the embassy. More than 200 were wounded or killed by the blast.

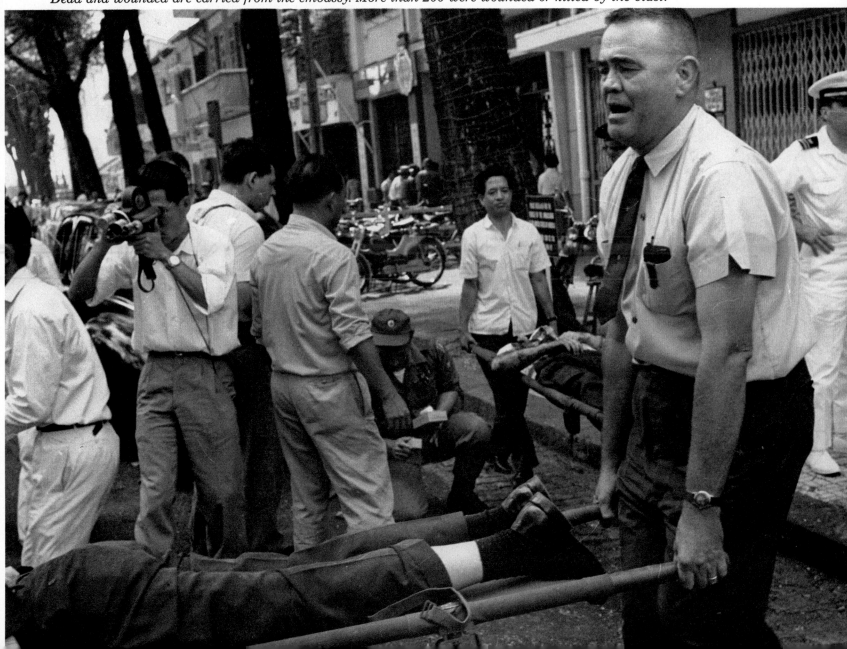

America Comes to Vietnam

The American buildup continued through the summer and fall, setting the stage for the first major battles with the North Vietnamese regulars who also had now entered the war. By the end of 1965, American troop strength soared to 181,000.

In addition to the 173rd Airborne Brigade, the American forces included units from such famed divisions as the 101st Airborne, the 1st Air Cavalry and the 1st Infantry.

Oriental boom towns with strips of restaurants, beer parlors, ice shops, laundries, jewelry stores and souvenir shops sprang up wherever U.S. bases were established. Merchants out to make a fast American buck hung out their signs for everything from toy costumed dolls to elephant skin wallets and tortoise-shell pocket combs.

Cam Ranh Bay was turned into a shopping center in the middle of the desert. In addition to its excellent natural harbor and the huge logistical complex that was being constructed there, the beautiful bay and beach provided the Americans with a natural recreation area.

The Chase Manhattan Bank and the Bank of America opened branches in Saigon to serve American personnel. The PX set up a plan under which servicemen could order an American auto for pickup in the United States with a

Recalling troop ships of the First and Second World Wars troops of the 1st Brigade, 101st U.S. Airborne Division look out on the large sandy expanses at Cam Ranh Bay in July, 1965.

Two Vietnamese work a jackhammer at Cam Ranh Bay. The United States employed thousands of Vietnamese to help construct its massive base system. At Cam Ranh Bay, a group of Vietnamese war widows dubbed the "tiger ladies" provided an efficient and productive work force despite their diminutive size (less than five feet tall and under 100 pounds).

Above: *Colonel James E. Simmons, commander of the 2nd Bridage, 1st Infantry Division, welcomes his troops ashore at Cam Ranh Bay. At its height, the base at Cam Ranh housed and employed nearly 20,000 U.S. servicemen and occupied and area over 15 miles long and nearly five miles wide.* Below: *Flags of the 101st Airborne are dipped in salute as the division arrives in Vietnam at Cam Ranh Bay. The members of the "Screaming Eagles" are identified by their distinctive shoulder patches.*

A line of boats await unloading in Cam Ranh harbor in January, 1966. From a single deep water pier in 1963, the Cam Ranh docking facilities eventually expanded to six piers capable of offloading up to four thousand tons of cargo per day. Below: Cam Ranh Bay, 1969.

down payment of $250. GIs were able to do their Christmas shopping through the PX's Mail-a-Gift catalog, with selections ranging from sporting goods to silverplate.

Inevitably, the expansion of U.S. forces and the attendant rapid infusion of billions of dollars in goods and material led to an equally rapid growth in black marketeering. In a two-month study, Associated Press reporters Fred Hoffman and Hugh Mulligan uncovered numerous cases of graft, theft and bribery. They found that hundreds of millions of American taxpayers' dollars were being siphoned off. A few of the individual scams and illegal practices they uncovered included:

—South Vietnamese "ghost battalions" with padded payrolls for "phantom soldiers" who were carried as present for duty but paid off their commanders so they could work elsewhere for the Americans for much higher pay.
—A stolen U.S. Army generator lighting a Saigon nightclub.
—U.S. irrigation pumps intended for the rice-growing Mekong Delta being used by privately owned car-wash stations.
—An entire boatload of beer stolen.
—A truck piled high with PX goods moving through a narrow alley in Saigon, where a wire strung overhead lops off the top packing cases.
—Counterfeit U.S. military scrip and bogus PX cards appearing almost as fast as the real thing.
—Pilferage by both American and Vietnamese, adding millions of dollars to the cost of projects undertaken by private U.S. construction firms such as air bases and the port at Cam Ranh Bay.

Corruption was not the only problem with the tremendous logistical buildup which accompanied the expansion of U.S. involvement. Colonel Charles Reidenbaugh served as an adviser in Xuan Loc province, east of Saigon. He expressed his views in a letter to Joyce Eakin of Mechanicsburg, Pennsylvania.

There is no magic date by which this war will be won. The public has become mesmerized with statistics—how many troops now in Vietnam? How big will the buildup be? Numbers are meaningless at this stage in the game. The question that should be asked is when and where do we need additional combat power to defeat the enemy. Not how many by number. The war will be won when the Viet Cong, the National Liberation Front, North Vietnam and the Chinese, and for that matter, the Russians, have come to the conclusion that continuing the war is no longer productive. What will it take to force them to such a conclusion? You are out of my field. I'm an infantryman, not a clairvoyant.

As America's involvement in Vietnam grew, so did antiwar sentiment in the United States. With more Americans being sent to Vietnam each day, more families became personally in-

58

Six U.S. Naval cargo ships unload supplies at Da Nang harbor in October, 1966. The shortage of deep-draft piers in Vietnam created a serious problem. At one point in 1965, 91 ships waited in Saigon harbor to be unloaded.

Above: *Troops walk along the beach at Cam Ranh Bay. The base contained a milk-recombining plant, a permanent laundry, a 2,000 bed hospital and two 10,000-foot runways.* Below: *U.S. Navy seamen explore the tiny fishing village at Cam Ranh.*

October 17, 1965. Marchers gather outside San Francisco City Hall to demonstrate against the war.

Above: *George Clark, board member of the Committee on Nuclear Disarmament addresses a crowd on the University of California at Berkely campus at a Vietnam protest rally. Below: November 11, 1965. Fort Devens, Massachusetts. Various peace organizations protest the United States' role in Vietnam outside Fort Devens military reservation.*

volved in the war. For the first time, many Americans questioned the reasoning behind the U.S. involvement.

Among the men serving in Vietnam, however, support still ran high. They were putting their lives on the line each day in service to their country, and they resented the nascent antiwar movement. Many expressed their resentment in the angry letters they sent home.

Private 1st Class Robert Felter, a 23-year-old Marine, wrote to his hometown newspaper, the Troy, New York, *Record.*

I wonder if they have ever been scared. I have been scared and still am scared, whether it's a sweep and clear operation or just a patrol. But I know it has got to be done and I do it. Maybe if they came over here and saw guys blown up by mines, getting hit by mortars or being shot, maybe then it would sink into their thick skulls what we are doing here to keep them free so they can go to college. I am writing this letter beside a candle and I hope you can read it. Thanks for listening.

Felter was killed six months after he arrived in Vietnam.

Captain Donald R. Brown of Annapolis, Maryland, adviser to the 2nd Battalion, 46th Vietnamese Regiment, dashes for cover at a hot LZ on a rice paddy 15 miles west of Saigon on April 4, 1965.

Another Marine, Corporal George Derieg, 19, of Alameda, California, sat in a bunker on Hill 268 overlooking rice paddies and the South China Sea near Da Nang as he was handed a letter from 16-year-old Kathy Truxal, of Columbus, Ohio. Derieg had written to the Oakland, California, *Tribune* saying that some young people at home "don't seem to realize why we're here." He said the letter was directed toward some students at the University of California in Berkeley who had demonstrated against U.S. involvement in the war. A story about his letter was printed in the Columbus *Dispatch,* where Kathy read about it. She responded to Derieg's angry complaint:

Our young people are more aware of this situation than you might think. In fact I would assume the majority of us are acutely aware of this situation. Even more so than many adults are. Do you know why? Well, I'll tell you. Our younger generation is going

59

to inherit that whole godforsaken war and its horrors and troubles. As you step down, we will step up and take over the responsibility of defending our rights and our country.... You are fighting for us, our rights, as well as fighting for them [the Vietnamese]. It is a foreign soil that you fight on, but not a foreign reason. You just remember this. I for one am behind you all the way. We all are one way or the other. We are prepared to give up our lives for our country just the way you fellows do over there.

Derieg wrote back a second letter:

Kathy's letter is like many I have received since I first wrote to my hometown newspaper. First of all, I'd like to apologize to Kathy and to the other people who think as we think. My letter was written to those who don't think we should be here in Vietnam. I tried to make them see what we here fighting see, what we feel and why we feel it. There is not a man here—be he a Marine, a sailor, or an Army soldier—that enjoys being here. The days are hot and long and at times quite nerve-racking. They may complain because of these conditions, but we stand together under our president and will continue to do what he asks of us. Working for him is working for ourselves. In this case we are helping a smaller country get up off

Poet Allen Ginsberg delivers a protest to the war at an anti-Vietnam demonstration in July, 1965.

Paratroopers of the U.S. 327th Airborne Battalion crouch under cover at the edge of a jungle clearing 13 miles northwest of Ben Cat. They are seeking VC snipers who fired on them as they landed.

its knees and fight against the communists.

Lance Corporal Terrance Melton, 20, of Phoenix, Arizona, who was in the same outfit as Derieg, was upset about a photograph the Arizona *Republic* ran of Berkeley students carrying a sign reading "Thirteen have gone to jail to end the war in Vietnam. What are you doing about it?"

Melton wrote to the newspaper.

Well, I'll tell you what we're doing about it. We live in tents with nothing but shady earth for our floor. When it rains, which is frequent, we live in the mud. We eat, but you can't call a constant diet of dehydrated pods really eating. We have all lost, on the average, 16 pounds. But is our morale low? No, it is not low. It is outstandingly high, even considering the little mail we receive. You know why? Because we are fighting for our beloved country that we may never see

again, and to protect our loved ones, and kids like you, so you can go to your dances, parties and these absurd protests.

Marine Lance Corporal Henry Bacich, the 19-year-old son of a Milwaukee church janitor, wrote the Milwaukee *Journal* protesting a sympathy march in that city for an Army officer convicted by a court-martial of disobeying orders to join a counter-guerrilla unit in Vietnam.

Do they realize that another man had to take his place? Do they have any sympathy for the others who are out in the jungle acting as advisers for the Vietnamese troops and is there any sympathy for the men who went into the Viet Cong infested territory and lost their lives? I sincerely hope these people will come to realize the importance of us being here and keep this thought in mind: If we don't stop the communists here, where will

Bottom row, far left: *June, 1965. Communist mortar shell explodes near U.S. compound in Dong Xoai. Twenty-one Americans were listed as wounded, dead or missing in this battle, which almost resulted in the first commitment of U.S. combat troops to battle in Vietnam.* Middle left: *Vietnamese rangers race toward VC positions during the battle for Dong Xoai, which*

Thousands of demonstrators march down Pennsylvania Avenue in Washington, D.C., towards the White House to protest U.S. policy in Vietnam.

tion only delayed the inevitable.

In August, American forces finally engaged in their first major combat—Operation Starlite. In an attempt to trap a Viet Cong regiment that was planning an attack on the U.S. installation at Chu Lai, 4,000 Marines moved by air and sea onto the Van Tuong Peninsula, 10 miles south of Chu Lai. In two days of sharp action the Marines cleared the peninsula. They reported 573 enemy dead. The Marines in turn had suffered 46 deaths and 204 wounded.

As that battle ended, a new North Vietnamese threat appeared in the Central Highlands. In October, a North Vietnamese army regiment encircled the Special Forces camp at Plei Me, part of the enemy's plan to cut the country in half by slicing through the Central Highlands to the coast. After a siege of six days, the South Vietnamese, with the help of the U.S. 1st Cavalry Division (Airmobile, better known as the 1st Air Cavalry), repelled the attack and

we stop them? Are these future leaders truly concerned with the actions here in Vietnam, or is it just another "come and go" fad, such as stuffing people into a phone booth or a small foreign car. If they are truly concerned, they would not be holding these foolish demonstrations. All I can say is that if these people would drop by an elementary school and visit a first or second grade classroom, they would hear children giving us more backing than themselves each morning just reciting our pledge of allegiance to the flag.

Letters such as these from soldiers serving in Vietnam sparked many Americans to express their support. Hundreds of greetings, many of them from children, were sent to the American troops as part of "Mail Call Vietnam," a project inspired by Dr. Richard Ornsteen and his wife, June, of Philadelphia, to "let our boys over there know how much we appreciate what they are doing." One

schoolboy wrote: "Teacher told me to write to the most important man I could think of—and that's you."

The War Begins: The Battle of the Ia Drang

The increase in U.S. combat personnel made a major confrontation with the enemy only a matter of time. In June, members of the U.S. 173rd Airborne Division nearly became the first to engage the enemy in a full-scale battle when 1,500 guerrillas attacked the district capital of Dong Xoai, 40 miles north of Saigon in III Corps. At the last minute, however, South Vietnamese Brigadier General Cao Van Vien, the commander of III Corps, decided to hold back the U.S. troops, explaining that "I think that the Viet Cong is deliberately trying to draw American units into this fight." His ac-

The strain of battle registers on the face of U.S. Army Sergeant Philip Fink of Mosheim, Texas. An adviser to the 52nd Vietnamese Ranger Battalion, Fink and his men bore the brunt of the fighting at Dong Xoai.

lasted four days. Middle right: *June 10, 1965. With the rest of his squad pinned down by communist machine gun fire, a Vietnamese ranger runs for cover across a soccer field at Dong Xoai.* Far right: *VC soldier peers from a bunker towards GVN troops during the battle for Dong Xoai.*

Above: *Sharpened bamboo sticks rise from the ground as U.S. Marines move through the brush on Van Tuong Peninsula during Operation Starlite. Starlite was a classic Marine operation, using both land and sea forces and utilizing an amphibious landing.* Below: *Smoke from U.S. tactical air strikes rises near the triangular Special Forces camp at Plei Me.*

secured the camp. Prior to the arrival of the U.S. combat troops, the South Vietnamese would have been content to have called an end to the engagement at this point. However, the United States, after several months of preparation, was now ready to flex its muscles and face the communists.

Intelligence reported that two NVA battalions were massing five miles to the west of Plei Me in the Ia Drang Valley. Major General Harry O. Kinnard, the commander of the 1st Air Cavalry, asked for and received permission from Westmoreland to seek out the enemy. On October 28, he initiated his operation.

Left: Unidentified wounded Marine helped to evacuation helicopter after he was pulled from a blasted tank on the Van Tuong peninsula, August 19, 1965. Helping their buddy are (left) Corporal James Williams of Craig, Colorado, and Corporal Frank T. Guilford, of Philadelphia. Below: November 15, 1965. Smoke from 750 pound bombs dropped by U.S. B-52 hangs over the Ia Drang Valley. Stretching along the Laos–South Vietnam border, the Ia Drang contained a major communist supply route.

B Company, 2nd Battalion, 7th Cavalry, fire through brush at VC snipers in the Ia Drang Valley.

This would be the first time U.S. troops would face North Vietnamese regulars.

For nearly a month, the U.S. and the NVA chased each other across the valley in encounters ranging in size from squads to battalions. More often than not, the encounters were short and bloody as each side took turns ambushing the other.

Unshaven member of the 1st Air Cav carefully advances through the Ia Drang with bayonet fixed.

"We were walking along at the center of the battalion and we started getting fire all of a sudden," said Staff Sergeant Miguel Seise of Augusta, Georgia. "It was coming from everywhere, the ground, the trees. Suddenly, everyone around me was getting hit and dying. I could hear screams all over the place. We fought and fought for what seemed hours. But it was no good. I told what was left of my men, and there weren't many, to pull back if they could. I told them they had a fifty-fifty chance of getting out. We started crawling away under terribly intense fire. We crawled two hundred and fifty yards, then started running. I never ran so fast before. We had to leave most of the wounded people behind. But we tried to help some of them by crawling with them. The ones we left behind were screaming in pain and fear. Someone shouted out, 'Don't leave me!' A lieutenant called out, 'Please shoot me! Please shoot me! I don't want them to get me!'"

U.S. troops emerged from the Ia Drang exhausted but victorious. They had lost 247 men and had 570 wounded in the month-long battle. The U.S. Command claimed that the three NVA regiments they had faced—the 33rd, 34th, and 66th—had suffered 1,500 dead before limping across the border into Cambodia.

One of the American advisers who had survived the battle of Plei Me, John Gill, a Marine staff sergeant, wrote his wife Mickie, in Port Huron, Michigan, after the battle.

Send me some seeds so that I can plant them. We want fresh vegetables to make a salad. Green onions, carrots, head lettuce, radishes, anything that will grow. My darling, I want a picture of the first snow, just so I'll know that somewhere in the world there's a place without steam, mud, slush and stink. It's only 9:45 a.m. and the temperature is already 104 degrees. The humidity is 97 percent. I've lost 22 pounds. We eat 24 hours a day. This jungle, there's no end to it. There's so much I want to talk about. Things have to get better, darling. They can't get worse.

With the smoke from a B-52 raid still clouding the air, 1st Air Cav soldiers advance towards North Vietnamese positions in the Ia Drang. Facing page: U.S. paratroopers rush to take up positions around Phouc Vinh airfield just south of Dong Xoai on June 13, 1965.

AGENT ORANGE

The planes, mostly twin-engine C-123 cargo transports, would take off before dawn. After circling at high altitudes, they would swoop down to almost 150 feet from treetop level, tempting targets for ground gunners. The slow-moving craft would then spray their loads on the Vietnamese countryside and return to base within five minutes, mission accomplished.

The C-123s were taking part in an operation code-named Ranch Hand. Begun on January 13, 1962, as an experiment sponsored by the Defense Department's Advanced Research Project Agency, Operation Ranch Hand was designed to deny ground cover to the guerrillas by killing the heavy jungle foliage that covered much of South Vietnam and shielded the guerrillas from aerial observation. A much smaller herbicide campaign was also carried out against crops in an attempt to deny food to the VC.

The most common herbicide used by the Air Force was Agent Orange (named for the color-coded orange stripe painted around the 55-gallon storage drum). In the next nine years, an estimated 12 million gallons of Agent Orange were spread over an area the size of the state of Connecticut. Most of the sprayings took place over remote, largely unpopulated areas known to be inhabited by the VC. Occasionally, the military also used the defoliant to clear areas surrounding U.S. bases.

Initially, criticism of the defoliation program was directed against the possible long-term damage being done to South Vietnam's ecology. In 1969, however, a study conducted by the Bionetic Research Laboratories was released by the Food and Drug Administration, reporting that one of Agent Orange's components, 2,4,5-T, caused malformations in test animals. On October 29, 1969, the White House announced a partial curtailment of the use of Agent Orange in Vietnam.

The following April, use of Agent Orange in Vietnam was suspended entirely after the Department of Agriculture decided to severely limit the chemical's use in the United States. The department's studies had indicated "that 2,4,5-T as well as its contaminant, dioxin, may produce abnormal developments in unborn animals." (In the summer of 1970, two brigades of the American Division continued to use Agent Orange

"Crop dusting" Vietnam-style. Three U.S. UC 123 Providers spray defoliants over a jungle-covered area in South Vietnam.

Before and after. An unsprayed mangrove forest 60 miles from Saigon and the remains of another mangrove forest five years after spraying.

Above: *August, 1965. U.S. Marines file out of the village of Cam Ne south of Da Nang Air Base after burning down nearly 100 huts. Soon after leaving the village which was believed to be a base area for local VC, the soldiers came under heavy sniper fire.* Below: *After a long winter, leaves again shade a lane outside the Village of Can Gio in South Vietnam. Three years earlier a massive defoliation campaign stripped the entire area bare.*

when their store of another herbicide, Agent Blue, ran out. However, the practice was soon stopped and the officers involved punished. All herbicide operations in Vietnam were stopped entirely on June 30, 1971.)

Vietnam veterans started to report what they believed to be Agent Orange-related illnesses in the late 1970s. More than 16,000 Agent Orange-related claims were filed by servicemen suffering from ailments including skin and liver diseases and cancer of soft tissue organs such as lungs, stomach and muscles. Complaints to the Veterans Administration described numbness and tingling of fingers, insomnia, change of personality, malformed children and a painful skin rash known as chloracne.

In 1979, the Environmental Protection Agency suspended use of Agent Orange in the United States following reports of increasing numbers of stillbirths in Oregon, where the chemical had been heavily used.

In 1983, the Air Force concluded a study of the 1,269 pilots and crewmen who participated in Operation Ranch Hand. The report stated that none of the crews had suffered an unusually high death rate. While discussing the report's findings, Major General Murphy Chesney, deputy Air Force Surgeon General, offered the following observation: "Do I worry as a physician because we used it? The answer is no. I say war is hell—you've got to win it. Agent Orange was a war agent. It was used to protect our ground troops. It saved millions of lives possibly—thousands, anyway —in Vietnam."

Many Vietnam veterans, however, contend that the Air Force study does not cover the largest and most seriously affected group among Vietnam veterans—ground troops. Unlike Ranch Hand units, ground units could not change clothes and bathe at the end of the day. Furthermore, ground units also drank water and ate food contaminated by the herbicide. Finally, many more ground troops than airmen were exposed to Agent Orange. One General Accounting Office report noted that 19,000 Marines were stationed near sprayed areas during one four-week period.

In 1982, Agent Orange victims filed a class-action suit on behalf of three thousand veterans, asking five chemical companies to establish a $44 million fund to compensate victims. The companies involved were Dow Chemical, Hercules, Diamond-Shamrock, Monsanto and Thompson-Hayward Chemical.

CHAPTER 6
THE GUTS OF THE WAR

The worst job in the world, [is] taking a kid's body home to his parents."—First Lt. Scott Low, 1966

Scott Low, like many of the GIs returning from Vietnam, was assigned the task of returning the bodies of dead soldiers to their families. And in 1966, there were more bodies returning from Vietnam than ever before.

In the first quarter of 1965, 71 Americans were killed in Vietnam; in the last quarter, 920; and by 1966, an average of 400 U.S. soldiers per month lost their lives there as they sought out the North Vietnamese and Viet Cong from the swamps of the Mekong Delta to the mountainous jungles along the demilitarized zone. The war they fought was not one of full-blown conventional battles. Rather, it consisted of small, vicious encounters, usually inconclusive, always bloody. This was a war of attrition, fought without fronts and without strategic objectives, against an enemy as difficult to find as he was to kill.

As 1965 began, the communists were steadily expanding their control over the countryside and their switch to larger-scale operations against South Vietnamese forces had produced victory after victory. However, with the South Vietnamese on the brink of defeat, the U.S. had stepped in to thwart the communist offensive.

Faced with the overwhelming logistical and firepower superiority of the United States, the communist leaders were forced to rethink their strategy. While maintaining their forces in large units, they decided upon a return to guerrilla tactics, adopting a waiting-game strategy.

At the end of 1965, the North Vietnamese leadership drew up a list of their goals for the following year. Heading that list was the number of U.S. casualties—dead and wounded—they wished to inflict: 50,000. Now as the guerrilla teams deployed around the country, they would lie in wait not to liberate or secure strategic locations, but to kill Americans.

Facing page: *June, 1965. Inscription on the helmet of this soldier from the 173rd Airborne Brigade sums up his feelings towards the war.* Above: *Medic Thomas Cole, a private first class from Richmond, Virginia, continues to tend another wounded soldier despite injury to his left eye. Cole was wounded in action between 1st Air Cav and NVA troops in 1966. (Photo by Henri Huet earned a Robert Capa Award in 1971.)*

HO CHI MINH TRAIL

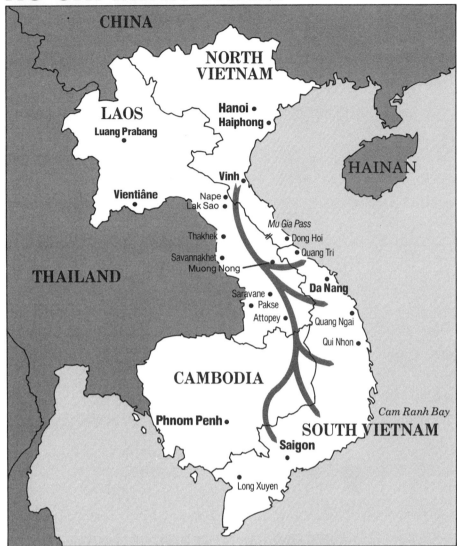

A single truck rarely ever made the full run; rather, the run was a system of transfers from point to point, using trucks, oxcarts and human hands. Some supplies were put in barges and barrels and floated downstream.

"As many as twenty transfers may take place," said one officer familiar with the workings of the network. "Following a box of ammunition through the Mu Gia Pass (between North Vietnam and Laos), it moves on a truck at night. The truck moves about eight miles, then pulls into a park covered by the thick jungle canopy. He unloads. During the next day, the ammunition is loaded to another truck. He moves sixteen miles, then unloads, and so on."

The B-52 strategic bombers, carrying up to 30 tons of bombs, made it difficult for the North Vietnamese to travel during the day, necessitating the system of relays to allow movement by night.

The shuttle system also allowed drivers to become more proficient and familiar with the section of the trail assigned them.

It was believed the North Vietnamese had a fleet of about 5,000 trucks, most of them Russian-made Zils, similar to American Ford trucks. There were two models, Model 130, a single-axle truck that could carry four tons of cargo, and Model 157, a six-wheel-drive vehicle that could carry six tons of supplies and had tires that could be inflated or deflated automatically from inside the cab to adjust to the terrain.

Other trucks came from East Germany, Poland, China and Czechoslovakia.

There were estimates that as many as 75,000 people worked on the trail network, including a coolie force of Laotian tribesmen and villagers.

At the height of the American efforts on the trail, between 300 and 400 Air Force, Navy and Marine combat aircraft were in action every day. About half of them attacked targets; the other half served as support, providing command and control planes, reconnaissance and refueling and storage. In addition, up to 30 B-52 strategic bombers hammered the network daily.

Still, supplies got through.

"It is essentially a jungle, a lot of mountains, a lot of places to hide, in caves and ravines," said one officer. "There are an inordinate amount of roads and alternate roads. Trying to hit a barrel in the water is not the easiest thing in the world."

The indispensable lifeline in the North Vietnamese supply operation to their forces fighting in South Vietnam was known as the Ho Chi Minh trail.

That maze of tangled routes threaded westward out of three North Vietnamese passes, through the mountains into Laos, then south and east through that country for 200 miles. It became one of the most important objectives of the United States in Indochina. For a time, most of the American air power in Southeast Asia was concentrated on it.

By choking off North Vietnamese supplies and troops moving southward along the trail, the United States hoped to buy time for the Vietnamization program and to reduce Hanoi's capabilities for waging war. Much of the plan to turn over air, logistics and other support activities to the South Vietnamese was dependent in part on the success of the bombing of the Ho Chi Minh trail.

After the overthrow of Cambodian Prince Norodom Sihanouk in March 1970 and the closing to the North Vietnamese of the Cambodian port of Kompong Som on the Gulf of Siam, the Ho Chi Minh trail was the communists' only alternative route for moving war material southward.

The Ho Chi Minh trail was actually a series of trails, dirt roads and river crossings stretching at least 30 miles wide and covering a 6,000-mile network. Much of it was covered by jungle. It reached southward 200 to 300 miles into Cambodia and South Vietnam.

The Ho Chi Minh trail was so complex that trucks sometimes seemed to disappear suddenly. One Air Force officer described it as a "spider web and another spider web lying on top of it and another and another."

"The North Vietnamese," he said, "are like broken-field runners moving in any direction they can to escape air attack and get supplies to their forces. They are ranging as far west as they can, and we're coming after them. The enemy can expect no sanctuaries from the air."

There were between 1,250 and 1,700 truck parks and storage areas on the trail.

Ambush

In early May, 1966, Private Reuben Morales, a 19-year-old Marine from La Puente, California, trudged through the thick jungle southwest of Da Nang. For the past three hours, Morales and the other 13 members of his patrol had searched vainly for any signs of the Viet Cong. They had seen nothing, but the soldiers knew otherwise. In the jungles of Vietnam, visible or not, death was always lurking. Crossing a rice paddy at one end of the valley, the patrol walked into a barrage of enemy fire.

"The first guy hit was the point man," said Morales. "Then they hit a corpsman and then a private on the

Top left: *Marines combine with an ARVN Ranger Company in the sweep through suspected Viet Cong country.* Above: *Inflated rubber boats "float" on the shoulders of paratroopers making their way through high elephant grass toward the Song Be River.*

Above: *Paratroopers from the 101st Airborne assault a hill near Dak To under cover of smoke grenades during June, 1966.* Below: *Member of the U.S. 25th Infantry shouts encouragement to his buddies as they return fire during a patrol north of Cu Chi on February 14, 1966. The area was known as "Hell's half acre."*

right flank. The radio was hit and we couldn't call the company. When someone tried to run, he was hit. A Filipino —he had only two days left to serve here—tried to make a run for it. He was hit in the back, but got up and started running again. Then he was hit again and fell. I knew he was running

for help. He fell three different times.

"I stood up after the second time. I was dizzy, but I could see the Viet Cong coming toward us. I wanted to take it standing up. The other guys who could stand stood up, firing away. The wounded were shooting, too.

"The Viet Cong? You could close your

Captured communist photo shows VC crossing a river in 1966.

Morales, blistering for three hours in the parched paddy under temperatures over 100 degrees, decided to make a move.

"As I started to crawl," he said, "I expected them to shoot me in the back. There was a Marine with his legs over the paddy wall. He said he couldn't move, and I told him I'd be back. I could see our troops across the field, but they were moving very slow. I came to another trooper from our squad, but he couldn't move his legs. And I saw three others, all of them face down. I guess they were dead."

Then Morales crawled over to Private First Class James Binkley, 19, of Ashland City, Tennessee, the other survivor. They started moving to where they could see the reinforcements kneeling. When they finally reached the other Americans, they waited for an evacuation helicopter after being given water and first aid.

"I ran to the helicopter," Morales said. "There was firing and a lot of confusion. Someone said a bullet hit the chopper's fuel line and we had to get out. I ran and dived into some weeds. I heard slugs flying over us. The crew told us the chopper was going to explode, and I ran again, just before it blew up. There were those other two guys wounded. I told them I'd be back. I wanted to bring them out. So did Binkley. We tried, but we couldn't."

Morales ran to a trench. Finally, a second helicopter flew in and evacuated him and Binkley.

eyes and not miss. I ran out of ammunition when the VC hit the first paddy wall, a low mound of dirt, and I was ready to start swinging my rifle when I got hit in the neck. I fell on my back, but I was not unconscious. I heard all the noises, the mortars and grenades.

"I opened my eyes and saw the Viet Cong shoot two other guys out in front of me on the second paddy wall. I heard them coming toward me and closed my eyes. They took my rifle, a grenade I had, and ammunition. Then one picked me up by the shirt to search me, but dropped me back.

"I was waiting, thinking, 'When will he pull the trigger?' More shooting started, and the two VC near me started walking away. When mortars opened up, I looked and saw them running back into the tree line. I heard another Marine calling, 'Corpsman! Over here! Over here!' And I heard our troops (the reinforcements) trying to get to us, but they couldn't. After a while the other Marine stopped hollering. I was scared. I thought we had been left."

Private First Class Lacey Skinner of Birmingham, Alabama, crouches in mud as heavy enemy fire pins his squad from the 1st Air Cav in a rice paddy near An Thi during fierce fighting in January, 1966. Facing page: U.S. Marines watch as an evacuation helicopter swirls through the dawn sky to pick up wounded. The Marines are fighting just south of the DMZ in Operation Prairie.

Above: *Armed with M-16s Air Force guards stand night watch from sandbagged bunkers along runway.* Right: *January 1967. New home of the U.S. Army Engineer Command HQ at Bien Hoa outside of Saigon.*

One of the problems facing the U.S. forces during 1965 and 1966, and indeed for the entire war, was their inability to initiate contact with the enemy. They continued to fight the war on the Viet Cong's terms. The static, defensive nature of the U.S. involvement during these years contributed greatly to the problem. Lacking either adequate troops or effective intelligence to actively seek out the enemy, U.S. troops were forced to wait for them to make contact.

As Billie Holmes, a 23-year-old Navy medical corpsman from Madison, Tennessee, discovered, this led to many sleepless and deadly nights. Late one afternoon in June 1966, Holmes and a group of 12 Marines had assumed defensive positions on a hill near Da Nang. Soon after nightfall, the Viet Cong attacked.

Again and again, scores of guerrillas drove up the hill oblivious to the Marines' fire and tactical air strikes called in by Holmes' platoon leader, Staff Sergeant Jimmie Howard, 36, of San Diego. Very quickly, he heard his first call to action. Several yards away from Holmes, a wounded Marine called out to the corpsman for aid. Under heavy fire, the young corpsman crawled to the injured soldier.

"Before I could ask him anything, a grenade came between us," Holmes said. As it went off, most of the force of it hit him in the head. "I was momentarily blinded and couldn't see. I

Following a Viet Cong ambush which killed 11 Vietnamese and one American, Army Sergeant Harold Lewis of Notus Idaho relaxes for a moment along a road near Binh Gia on January 4, 1965. Even after the arrival of combat troops, advisers continued to play an important role.

was wounded by shrapnel in the back of my right leg, left hand, eye and nose. My ears were ringing real bad. Finally, I blacked out.

"I came to and the wounded man was being dragged away by two Viet Cong. They dragged him only about three to four feet away from me. I could partially see them from the grass. I could hear them going through his pockets and cartridge belt. I heard him moaning and then a second later I heard a shot. They shot him in the face.

"Maybe a couple of minutes later, one of the Viet Cong started crawling up toward me. As he reached out to grab hold of my shirt, one of our men shot across me and hit him in the face. There were maybe three or four more of them right in the same spot. When the one was shot, the other three or four backed down the slope."

Throughout the night, the Viet Cong continued the attack, and the Marines continued to hold. Despite being wounded in the back, Sergeant How-ard manned the radio, directing jets on strafing and bombing runs against VC positions.

"We killed some of the Viet Cong at close range," said Howard. "One of my corporals killed two of them with his field knife before he died. At the end we only had eight to twelve rounds of ammunition left. A couple of times the Viet Cong yelled at us in real good English: 'Marines, you die in an hour!' We yelled back: 'You bastards ain't got us yet!' I told my men to give them a horse laugh and we did."

Finally, as dawn approached, the communists broke off the attack, melt-ing back into the jungle to attack an-other group of Marines on another night. Of the 18 Marines who defended that hill, five were killed and 11 others were wounded.

Initially, the Viet Cong had been un-able to offset the tremendous edge in mobility and support which the United States enjoyed through its helicopters. Although the United States had to wait

Top: *Until it was replaced by the faster, more heavily armed Huey series, the CH-21 pictured here was the workhorse in South Vietnam. The slow, banana-shaped helicopters proved susceptible to ground fire and broke down frequently in the hot jungle climate.* Bottom left: *U.S. Marine door gunners look out from their H-46 Sea Knight. Developed for the Marines in 1959, the Sea Knight was capable of carrying up to 25 combat troops.* Bottom right: *CH-47 Chinooks await assembly at U.S. base at Qui Nhon. The versatile troop carriers were capable of carrying up to 65 troops.* Facing page: *A big lift for allied sweep in Vietnam. A helicopter lifts a 155mm Howitzer atop a 1,700-foot high hill near the Loatian border.*

Men of the 25th Infantry Division prepare to board a squad of Hueys (Bell UH-1D or UH-1Hs). The Huey could carry up to eight men. These troops are preparing to assault into Cambodia. The Huey was the workhorse of the Vietnam war, carrying troops, providing cover and operating as assault craft against communist positions.

April, 1967. U.S. Marines carry wounded to evacuation helicopters during battle near Binh Son, 20 miles south of Da Nang. The helicopter saved many lives during the Vietnam war because of its ability to speed the wounded to hospitals. Facing page: Sea Knight crashes in Song Ngan valley along the DMZ, killing Marine (foreground) as the blades break off on landing. Most of the helicopter crashes resulted from poor maintenance or pilot error.

First Lieutenant Joseph Burn (left) of Anniston, Alabama, carries medical supplies to treat civilians in Ap Co Co in the Mekong Delta as part of civic action program in 1963. Burn is assisted by Sergeant First Class Wilford Hayden of Portsmouth Virginia. The helicopter gave the U.S. forces in Vietnam a mobility unknown to any other army in the history of warfare.

for the Viet Cong to attack, they were able to call in reinforcements quickly enough to turn the tide in many engagements. The guerrillas, however, quickly developed several methods of countering the U.S. advantage. One tactic they employed was to attack a single U.S. unit and then wait to ambush the inevitable helicopter support. As Frank Faulkner, an Army correspondent with the 1st Brigade, 101st Airborne Division, learned, it could be a very effective tactic.

On a hot February day in 1966, the 21-year-old native of Springfield, Massachusetts, joined another correspondent, Jack Vaughn, on board a Medical Evacuation helicopter (medevac). They were heading for two U.S. platoons that had been mauled by the NVA during an operation along the central coast. Even before landing, Faulkner felt uneasy.

"This crew was visibly shaken," said Faulkner. "It turned out they had been shot down about three and a half hours earlier. The chopper had burned. The crew was picked up by a gunship. They went back and got another helicopter. And the four-man crew just got back in it and they just kept flying missions. They didn't even go through the debriefings or the paperwork of being shot down. We got on with them and

flew over the still-burning wreck of their helicopter.

"We hit a hot LZ [landing zone]. I got off and ran and I dropped the camera. As soon as I felt the camera fall off my web gear, I just sort of let my knees go and slid as though I was sliding into second base. And when I did that, the whole five feet in front of me, clods of dirt from the ground just started flying. Someone had been tracking me with a machine gun. I just happened to slide as they were squeezing the trigger, and it missed me.

Army correspondent Frank Faulkner.

That was when I realized how bad this LZ was.

"I crawled back, I got the camera. Jack and I managed to get over by this house that was burning. And finally we linked up with the Americans who were trying to hold this small perimeter.

"They had two platoons from Charlie Company and the platoons at that time were still running about forty, forty-five people. And out of the two platoons they had something like thirty-eight casualties between dead and wounded. They had been cut just about right in half.

"The Tiger Force was brought in. It was run by a lieutenant who was twenty-three years old. They were called the Tiger Force because they wore tiger fatigues; the rest of us wore the regular green jungle fatigues.

"As the Tiger Force came up, the fire shifted off us, and we tried to crawl down this dried creek bed and use light antitank weapons against reinforced machine gun bunkers.

"The machine gun fire started to build between the Americans and the North Vietnamese. Finally, the machine gunners just held the triggers down, firing everything they had all at once, just burning the barrels out. It was just a fantastic drum roll, something I'd never hear in Vietnam afterward in the two and a half years more I spent over there.

"The Tiger Force charged the machine gun bunkers. It was thirty-five or forty guys, no more, maybe less. Most were cut down. As some of them stopped to help their friends, the sergeant yelled out, 'Don't mind the bodies, just keep moving.' I never thought they would make it to where the machine guns were. I couldn't tell from where I was how many of them made it to the machine gun placements.

"The ones who survived the charge jumped in the holes. They were out of ammunition because they had fired it all charging over and they jumped in the holes with bayonets and rifle stocks and it was over like that."

The Other War

Not all of the U.S. troops sent to Vietnam fought a war of ambushes and firefights. Many of the soldiers sent to Vietnam were logistical personnel. They worked and lived in the world known as the news area. For many of them, the real enemy was boredom and loneliness, not the Viet Cong.

Weary member of the 173rd Airborne relaxes on his pack following a week of patrolling near Song Be.

Bob Sullivan, a 21-year-old Air Force MP from Marshfield, Massachusetts, stationed in Da Nang, wrote home to his fiancée, Eileen O'Neill, describing that life. He affectionately addressed her as "Bean."

August 25, 1966

Dear Bean:

Received your tape this morning and I was very surprised at seeing a small white box in #480. Instead of going to work, I drove down to the hut and heard your voice. I had forgotten what you sounded like but it is fresh in my memory now. As you spoke, I could see your expressions and the crinkle in your nose. I was smiling from ear to ear. After this past week, I thought I couldn't smile again, but your voice proved me wrong.

Tonight I had plans of returning your tape, but as usual, it is busy with troops in and out. My bunk mate is usually drunk at the club but for some reason he went on the wagon tonight. I have very poor Irish luck. Sunday I will be off and damn sure there will be a few hours of peace and quiet. Between the hours of six and eight, it is impossible to tape as the jets scream off the runway four at a time in 10-minute intervals heading for their targets up north. I won't miss that ear shattering noise at all. . . .

When I was a civilian I was hard to wake up but those days are over. Six-thirty sharp and I am wide awake on Sunday. Boy, that burns me up. During the night, I wake up six or seven times only to fall into a restless sleep. The next time those rockets hit, I am not going to be caught in my bunk as I was last time. When you hear that frightening shrill whistle of the rocket, you have exactly three seconds to spill under your bed. [My] good friend received a Dear John from his girl today. He is really taking it hard. They were supposed to be married September 16. Boy, I can almost feel the hurt he is going through. That's a horrible thing to do to someone over here.

I miss you, Bean. Thank you for the tape.
Much Love,
Bob

One last letter home. Just before his unit lands at Da Nang a young soldier writes home from the U.S.S. Upshua. Below: The most fearsome weapon from an arsenal of fearsome weapons, the B-52's were almost as effective as a psychological weapon—instilling fear in the communists and confidence in the allies—as they were as support bombers.

A member of the 1st Battalion, 9th Infantry, 1st Air Cav, has to make a quick dash for cover as an NVA sniper zeroed in on him while he was cleaning his weapon. The dismantled weapon is in his right hand.

With the arrival of U.S. combat troops in 1965, the focus of the U.S. effort shifted from training and advising the South Vietnamese to taking control and fighting the war. This shift added another obstacle to what was already an increasingly difficult task.

Captain Carlton Holland, a 36-year-old Army adviser with 18 years of military service already behind him, found it a frustrating experience. After a particularly disastrous operation, he expressed his dissatisfaction in a letter home to his wife in Junction City, Kansas.

"My four-day operation was uneventful and maddening, working with the Popular Forces," he wrote. "They are the dumbest laziest weakest, unpatrioticist I have ever seen . . . time and mis-sion were devoted to waiting for the Popular Forces and going after them when they got lost. Well, they got paid the day we got back and now they have 30 deserters—that leaves 46 in the company. I wish I could take some of those soldiers and just live in the hills and train them myself."

Holland's problems were not restricted to his own troops. The communists had singled out U.S. advisers as prominent targets. "The Viet Cong in this district have had assassins in town after me," he wrote his wife in February 1966. Although he would welcome the opportunity to face the enemy, he said, he knew he had to be on his guard at all times. Communist agents had infiltrated South Vietnamese units in increasing numbers, and Holland recognized the danger of his situation.

"They [his South Vietnamese guards] change too much—new ones every couple of days. I sleep with my automatic under my right hip. It is now 3:30 a.m. on February 7. I can't sleep. I'm hot and sweaty, feet cold and cramping. I'm writing with candlelight but the wind is going to blow it out. The rats are very bad tonight. These damned rats; I have to keep my feet up, they are running across them. I got my orders for the States, 45 days leave and report to Fort Bragg. How can mosquitoes fly in so much wind?"

Later that month, on the same day Holland's letter arrived, the Army notified his wife that he had been killed in action along with two other advis-

THE AIR WAR

On March 2, 1965, Major General Joseph H. Moore dispatched 25 F-105 fighter-bombers and 20 B-57 bombers on a bombing mission over North Vietnam, part of a new operation called Rolling Thunder. Originally the Rolling Thunder campaign was designed to accomplish three objectives: first, to raise South Vietnamese morale; second, to force the North Vietnamese to give up their support of the insurgency in the south, and third, to improve the U.S. bargaining position if and when negotiations started. Ultimately, it achieved none of these goals.

Although the bombing of North Vietnam temporarily improved South Vietnamese morale, it failed to convince the North Vietnamese to stop supporting the insurgency (if anything, the bombing only stiffened the north's resolve to continue) and the North Vietnamese Government consistently refused to allow the United State to use the bombing as a bargaining chip in negotiations.

Despite the massive scale of the bombing (between 1965 and 1968 U.S. planes dropped more than 605,000 tons of bombs on North Vietnam), the United State failed to seriously impede the north's ability to supply the insurgents in the south.

April, 1965. Marine Corporal R.G. Grice of Raleigh, North Carolina, sends a personal message to the Viet Cong on the side of this 250-pound bomb. From 1965 to 1968 alone, U.S. aircraft dropped more than 2.1 million tons of bombs on South Vietnam.

U.S. Air Force F-100 Supersabre from the 429th Tactical Fighter Squadron at Bien Hoa drops its load on a VC target near Biew Hoa. The type of ordnance ranged from incendiary bombs to fragmentation bombs. Below: The remains of the Lang Met Highway Bridge, 45 miles north east of Hanoi. U.S. F105s used massive 3,000-pound bombs to destroy the span.

An attack by U.S. Navy Skyhawks on a North Vietnamese train near the village of Vinh sends smoke billowing hundreds of feet into the air.

The shadow of a Navy reconnaissance jet passes near the wreckage of a North Vietnamese PT boat, one of five destroyed by planes from the carriers U.S.S. Hancock and U.S.S. Midway in a battle 50 miles north of the 17th parallel.

Smoke spews from the Nam Binh petroleum oil storage tanks 40 miles southeast of Hanoi. The attack, by aircraft from the U.S.S. Oriskany on July 2, 1965, marked the closest air strike to Hanoi since the beginning of Rolling Thunder.

Four F-105s attack a naval repair station in North Vietnam. The explosions are from two 750-pound bombs.

April 30, 1965. Forty tons of conventional bombs left this North Vietnamese military supply depot at Linh Dong a smoldering ruin.

ers when the Viet Cong overran the town of Duc Phong, 100 miles northeast of Saigon. In two months, he would have been heading home to be with his wife and three children.

As the United States continued to pour funds into the war effort, each day more and more bodies of American soldiers were flown home. Still, most Americans, including the soldiers themselves, continued to support the war. In 1966, Richard Marks, a 19-year-old Marine from New York City who would be killed several months later, wrote to his mother.

"I don't like being over here," he told her, "but I am doing a job that must be done—I am fighting an inevitable enemy that must be fought—now or later.... I am fighting to protect and maintain what I believe in and what I want to live in—a democratic society. If I am killed while carrying out this mission, I want no one to cry or mourn for me. I want people to hold their heads high and be proud of me for this job I did."

As 1966 ended, American resolve to continue the war remained firm. Still, the end was not in sight, and no one could say for certain when it would be over. What was certain, however, was that more Americans were on their way to Vietnam and many of them would die there.

Facing page: *Private First Class Benjamin Arkward from York, Pennsylvania.* Top: *A U.S. Marine waits in a bunker at Con Thien near the DMZ.* Bottom: *December, 1966. After reading a letter from home, an infantryman from the U.S. 4th Infantry Division holds his hands over his head.*

CHAPTER 7
SEARCH AND DESTROY

By the beginning of 1967, the American troop level in Vietnam had risen to 400,000 as a steadily increasing flow of U.S. men and matériel poured into the country. As the U.S. force grew and the South Vietnamese continued to suffer heavy casualties—nearly one infantry battalion per week—the United States, under the guidance of General Westmoreland, gradually assumed more and more of the burden of the war. (By the end of 1966 the United States had already suffered more than 5,000 dead and 30,000 wounded.)

Now Westmoreland prepared to begin the "big war." The limited war tactics of 1965 and 1966 would be discarded. 1967 would be the year of the large operations, the year of search and destroy.

Operation Cedar Falls

Operation Cedar Falls, the first major search-and-destroy operation of 1967, was launched on January 8. Its objective was an area known as the "Iron Triangle," a Viet Cong stronghold situated between Route 13 and the Saigon River, 20 miles northwest of Saigon. Described by MACV officials as a "dagger pointed at Saigon," the 60-square-mile tract of dense jungle, underground tunnels and rubber plantations, some long-abandoned, contained the headquarters for the Viet Cong's Military Region IV.

Left: *U.S. Marine from the 3rd Battalion, 4th Marines crouches in the entrance to a pagoda in a village along the Ben Hai river in the DMZ.* Above: *Lieutenant General William Westmoreland visits troops in the field.*

Infantryman from the 1st Battalion, 2nd Infantry Division, keeps his eyes peeled for snipers in the Thanh Dien Forest north of the "Iron Triangle" area. Below: A heavy Patton tank destroys a VC bunker in the Iron Triangle during Operation Cedar Falls.

Members of the village of Phu Huu are trained by a government pacification cadre to protect their village from VC attacks.

Above: *Government political officer leads village youth in singing patriotic songs.*
Below: *At the village of Binh Duong, 15 miles north of Saigon, a South Vietnamese Army band plays for villagers as part of pacification efforts.*

In the weeks prior to the operation, 15,000 U.S. troops were carefully deployed in a rough horseshoe around the area. All of the moves were coordinated to appear as routine operations, in an attempt to deceive the VC. Also, no word of the operation was given to the South Vietnamese to limit the chances of an intelligence leak.

The pre-positioned troops formed the anvil, one-half of the hammer-and-anvil tactic commonly used in U.S. search-and-destroy operations. With the anvil in place, the hammer, a second force of troops, would sweep through the open end of the horseshoe, forcing any guerrillas inside toward the anvil.

At 7:45 a.m., the first phase of Cedar Falls began. Flying in tight formation, 60 troop-carrying helicopters swept southward from the U.S. base at Dau Tieng. Their destination, 19 miles away, was the village of Ben Suc, which had been singled out as a major base of communist activity. At exactly 8:00 a.m., the choppers cleared the trees surrounding the village, taking only minimal groundfire. As they swooped in to land, the villagers looked on, bewildered.

Immediately, the 420 men of the 1st Battalion, 26th Infantry (known as the Blue Spaders), under the command of Lieutenant Colonel Alexander M. Haig, leapt from the helicopters and sped to secure the village. Five minutes later, air and artillery strikes pounded the woods to the north in an effort to prevent any Viet Cong from escaping. At 8:30 a.m., more troops were landed to the south of the village blocking that direction.

While chaos reigned on the ground, South Vietnamese officers, flying in U.S. helicopters equipped with loudspeakers, circled over Ben Suc urging the villagers to cooperate.

"You are surrounded by the Republic of South Vietnam and allied forces. Do not run away or you will be shot as VC. Stay in your homes and wait for further instructions."

After securing the area, the U.S. soldiers began to evacuate the town. Long a Viet Cong stronghold, Ben Suc had resisted all attempts at pacification. The local villagers actively supported the guerrillas, providing food, shelter, manual labor and anything else they needed. The only alternative, as far as the United States could see, was to level the village.

The U.S. troops helped to evacuate the nearly 6,000 inhabitants of the village along with their livestock and other possessions. Long columns of frightened women and crying children shuffled down the rutted clay roads, carrying their meager belongings of pots and pans, bedding and family keepsakes, their thatched-roof homes

TUNNEL RATS

"I kind of enjoy it; it breaks the routine."

Specialist 4 James Fedarko, a member of the 1st Battalion, 503rd Airborne Infantry, 173rd Airborne Brigade, was explaining why he volunteered for one of the more dangerous missions in Vietnam: searching out the enemy underground in their complex tunnel systems.

The "tunnel rats," as the men who searched out the tunnels were called, played an important role in Vietnam, where almost any hamlet could conceal a communist tunnel system. In 1967, one U.S. major commented that "here [Vietnam], occupation on the ground means nothing, unless you destroy the underground tunnels one by one."

This was the task that these men faced. The tunnel rats had to contend with everything from poisonous scorpions and bats to booby traps and lurking VC. All of them earned the respect of their fellow soldiers for carrying out their dirty and dangerous assignments.

In this instance, during Operation Cedar Falls, Charlie Company had found a tunnel that started with a shaft 10 feet deep. Fedarko, a native of Philipsburg, Pennsylvania, volunteered to go in.

Crawling down to the first level, he found a trapdoor; he dropped through it to a second level and, after crawling a few more feet, found another trapdoor. At this point, he decided to return to the first level. Carrying a pistol and a headset radio connected by wire to a radio aboveground, he checked the tunnel for booby traps, following his flashlight

A U.S. Marine fires his rifle into a bomb shelter in an attempt to flush out Viet Cong who may be hiding during an attack on the village of Chan Son on August 2, 1965.

Pistol cocked at the ready, Marine Corporal William G. Cox of Jackson, Mississippi, emerges from a tunnel in the Batangan Peninsula in South Vietnam. Controlled by the Viet Cong since 1964, the area contained a maze of bunkers, tunnels and arms caches.

beam down the zigzagging, dirt corridors, only 3 feet wide and 4 feet high.

After crawling 150 yards, he saw someone sleeping by a rucksack.

"The light woke him up to see who was coming," he remembered. "I shot three times. I think I hit him in the chest. He started to crawl off. There were others in there, too. I could hear them. I figured it was more than I could handle, and I came back up."

As was often done in cases like this, tear gas—composition CS, a powderlike, riot control agent—was blown into the tunnels using portable turbines in an attempt to smoke out the VC remaining in the tunnel. The next day, Specialist 4 Eugene Williams of Washington, D.C., and Dennis Doherty of New York City put on gas masks and took up the search.

They crawled past concrete doors leading off to the sides over trapdoors, and by branch tunnels, exploring 350 yards of tunnels. All the while, they kept a keen eye out for booby traps.

"You have to watch for those booby traps," Williams said. "It's like chasing someone through their own house. They know where they're going—but you don't."

Eventually, Charlie Company had to give up the chase. After the tunnel rats emerged, a demolition team placed explosives inside the tunnel and blew it up.

The complexity and durability of the tunnel systems amazed many Americans. Many tunnels had with-

stood B-52 strikes, and others contained fully operational surgical rooms, equipped with portable electric generators to provide light and power. After climbing out of one mazelike complex of tunnels, one tunnel rat offered a piece of grudging admiration: "You got to hand it to those little guys. They've been working on this a long time."

During Cedar Falls, the men of the 196th Light Infantry Brigade, commanded by Brigadier General Richard T. Knowles, stumbled upon one of the most extensive tunnel systems of the war. Entering head first through a small tunnel shaft, tunnel rats descended 16 feet to the tunnel floor. After finding and defusing numerous booby traps, they penetrated 600 yards into the tunnel complex and still had not found the end. Finally, they discovered a treasure trove of supplies, weapons and documents. Especially important were the documents found, which included the plans for a suicide guerrilla attack made the previous December 4 on Tan Son Nhut Air Base, and French and American maps and diagrams of hotels and billets that housed Americans in Saigon. In addition, they also found medical supplies, typewriters, rifles, pistols and 18 graves.

Following the discovery, General Knowles lauded the find, calling it "by far the most important one yet. This was his headquarters." For the tunnel rats it was just another day's work.

A soldier from the U.S. 1st Infantry Division's 3rd Brigade sets fire to a hut on the Michelin Rubber Plantation. The hut complex was used by the VC.

Near Tam Ky, a soldier from the 1st Air Cav flings a basket of rice into a burning house after an old woman retrieved it from the building.

Members of the 25th Infantry Division during Operation Malheur, sift through a VC village which they have just destroyed in Quang Ngai Province.

American soldier searches through the smoldering ruins of a Vietnamese farmhouse in the Mekong Delta.

burning behind them. Bulldozers and demolition teams moved in to complete the destruction. The first area they cleared, Briar Patch, was located in the southwest corner of the village.

"I guess it was about twenty acres of scrub brush," said Lieutenant Colonel Joseph M. Kiernan, commander of the engineer battalion. "The place was so infested with tunnels that as my dozers would knock over the stumps of trees, the VC would pop out from behind the dozers. We captured about . . . six or eight VC one morning. After the civilians were taken from the town, we went through and methodically knocked down the homes . . . tunnels were

through the whole area. . . . "

To complete the destruction, demolition teams planted 10,000 pounds of explosives in a large hole scooped out near the center of Ben Suc. Using a chemical fuse, they detonated the explosives, hoping to destroy any undiscovered tunnels.

The destruction of Ben Suc was indicative of the thinking behind the search-and-destroy strategy. These operations were not designed to find and kill the Viet Cong but rather to destroy their logistical base and to deny them access to his biggest resource, the people.

"If we were looking for the Viet Cong

main force, we wouldn't have gone here," said an officer from the 1st Infantry Division. "The object of this is not to kill Viet Cong. It is to remove the population from the enemy's control."

In the 19 days which the operation lasted, U.S. troops scoured the Iron Triangle, seeking out and destroying the extensive logistical system which the enemy had built up there. Nearly 500 tunnels stretching over 12 miles were uncovered and destroyed. Hundreds of weapons and thousands of rounds of ammunition were captured along with enough rice to feed 13,000 troops for a year. Also, nearly 500,000 pages of documents, including dia-

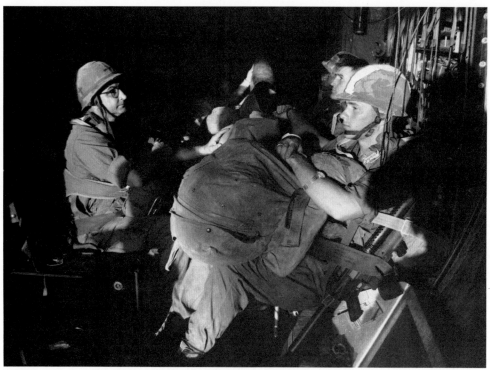

Major Xavier Gaglielo, Catholic chaplain from New York City, prays for a moment just prior to parachuting into War Zone C.

grams of U.S. billets in Saigon and outlines of terrorist attacks, were discovered, providing further evidence that this was the enemy's Military Region IV headquarters. Finally, the most obvious result of the operation was the 11 square kilometers of land stripped by the bulldozers and Rome Plows (these were specially designed bulldozers equipped for heavy-duty land clearance).

Less than a month after Cedar Falls, the United States mounted an even larger search-and-destroy operation —Operation Junction City. On the morning of February 22, 45,000 American troops, under the operational con-

trol of the 25th Infantry, formed a cordon around a Viet Cong base camp located in War Zone C northwest of Saigon near the Cambodian border.

Following a B-52 bombing run, paratroopers from the 503rd Airborne Brigade, attached to the 173rd Airborne Brigade, parachuted from 16 C-130 transports. This was the first major combat jump for the United States since Korea. As the 845 men of the 503rd floated to earth, five more brigades were helilifted into position. Again, as with Cedar Falls, the primary tactic employed would be the hammer and anvil.

Initially, U. S. units experienced only

light contact as the Viet Cong seemed content to avoid the Americans. A month into the operation, however, the guerrillas decided to fight back. On March 31, Lieutenant Colonel Haig led his battalion of Blue Spaders on a search-and-destroy operation near the village of Ap Gu.

While searching the woods northwest of the battalion's perimeter, a reconnaissance platoon spotted small signs hanging from the trees written in English warning the Americans not to go beyond that point. The Viet Cong had been expecting them.

As the recon patrol moved further north, they made contact. For the remainder of the afternoon, the 1st Battalion, 26th Infantry engaged the Viet Cong seeking to extricate the besieged recon patrol. Finally, in late afternoon, the patrol was rescued and the battalion established a defensive perimeter for the night.

Early the next morning the VC resumed the attack. At 5:00 a.m., Viet Cong mortar rounds began pounding all around the camp. Lieutenant Colonel Haig immediately recalled the troops manning listening posts outside the camp's perimeter. On their way back, the Americans accidentally hit their own trip flares, revealing their position to the waiting guerrillas.

"An [enemy] automatic weapon opened up on them, and I fired my M-79," said Private First Class William Trickett. "I believe I hit and silenced her. [The VC] came on in and wound up in the First Platoon area. It was a mixup after dark. The next thing we know, they're sprawling all over the field. Some way or another they came through our trip flares and were already in the field digging positions.

" . . . We lost one of our machine guns that was hit by a mortar. The other one kept firing, but considering the people we had on the listening post and everything, our positions were just under strength. We just got hit. They realized our weakness and came through us."

Captain George A. Jones, the battalion operations officer, said the Viet Cong walked right through the American artillery and mortar fire.

"They just kept coming, so we knew we had a very large force out there," he said. "Charlie Company was fighting hand to hand in the bunkers as was our Bravo Company. . . . We organized about seventy-five meters back . . . consolidated the line, and held."

The Blue Spaders reported finding nearly 500 Viet Cong bodies among their defenses after the fighting had ended. Seventeen Americans were killed and 102 were wounded.

At midnight on May 14, Operation Junction City ended. The U.S. Military Command said American forces had

U.S. soldiers take up defensive positions around the rim of a bomb crater caused by B-52 airstrikes in War Zone C during Operation Junction City.

killed nearly 3,000 Viet Cong troops. American losses were 282 men killed and 1,576 wounded.

Despite the impressive statistics racked up by the U.S. forces during Cedar Falls and Junction City, the search-and-destroy operations aroused controversy. Ultimately, they proved ineffective, often taking a heavy toll in American lives and alienating the civilian population from the Saigon government.

"One of the discouraging features of both Cedar Falls and Junction City,"

Left: U.S. engineers clear a Special Forces camp in War Zone C during operation Junction City in April, 1967. Involving nearly 45,000 U.S. troops, Operation Junction City was the largest operation of the war to that point. Below: Vietnamese civilians and members of the 3rd Brigade, 4th U.S. Division view the bodies of Viet Cong soldiers killed during an encounter with the 4th in War Zone C.

said Lieutenant General Bernard W. Rogers, "was the fact that we had insufficient forces, either U.S. or South Vietnamese, to permit us to continue to operate in the Iron Triangle and War Zone C and thereby prevent the Viet Cong from returning. In neither instance were we able to stay around, and it was not long before there was evidence of the enemy's return. Only two days after the termination of Cedar Falls, I was checking out the Iron Triangle by helicopter and saw many persons wandering around on foot."

The War Heats Up

As 1967 dragged on, the war continued to grow and intensify. U.S. troop strength reached 450,000 and U.S. casualties tripled. Rather than quell communist activity, the United States' expansion of the war had induced a reciprocal response from the communists. More and more U.S. patrols and installations came under attack.

One morning in October, two companies and a headquarters group from the U.S. 1st Infantry Division moved out from their night defensive positions in the thick jungles 40 miles northwest of Saigon. They did not have far to go. Nearby, 200 Viet Cong troops lay in wait, their camouflage blending in with the thick brush and treetops.

As the American troops moved into the open, only 50 feet away, the guerrillas opened fire. Machine gun and rifle fire ripped through the Americans from every side. A company commander tossed a hand grenade into one Viet Cong machine gun position. Moments later, a Claymore mine blew up in his face.

"They were set up and waiting just like a cat getting ready to jump," said First Sergeant José Valdez, 35, of Velarde, New Mexico. "We concentrated on breaking contact so we could bring artillery in.

"After my company commander got wounded, he called for me to take over. I was on the radio, trying to tell my men to break contact and pop smoke grenades in front of them to mark their positions and make sure air and artillery wasn't going to fall on top of them.

"At the same time, I was trying to get the wounded moved away from the fighting. What I had in mind was regrouping the company. We started to receive fire in the area where the wounded men were, so I decided to move again back toward our night position perimeter."

"There was nothing really to get behind, nowhere to hide," said Specialist 4 James Schultze, 19, of New York City. "They were just on all sides of us. It was a perfect ambush. You could just catch a glimpse of one or two of them. They were very well camouflaged. I

Top left: *A U.S. Air Force CH-3C (Air Force equivalent of the Navy Sikorsky HH-3E "Jolly Green Giant") delivers injured Marines to a field ambulance at a helipad at Da Nang.* Top right: *A wounded Viet Cong soldier is carried into the emergency room of the 2nd Surgical Hospital near Chu Lai in the northernmost sector of Vietnam. The only U.S. Army Hospital in the I Corps Zone, it operates as a medical*

depot for 18 units in the area. Bottom: *In an effort to increase medical facilities in Southeast Asia, the U.S. Air Force developed this completely air-transportable hospital consisting of prefabricated metal modules. The units were moved individually and then connected to form the hospital. A complete modern hospital could be built in 30 days. In emergencies, a facility could be put together within hours.*

never heard so much fire in my whole life."

Fifty-eight Americans were killed and 61 were wounded. More than 100 Viet Cong were reported killed.

It was a sunny Wednesday afternoon in December when two platoons from A Company, 4th Battalion, 12th Infantry, moved into the jungles 30 miles north of Saigon, searching for the site from which mortars had been fired into their camp the night before.

As was the custom, one of the chaplains accompanied the infantrymen. It was a good time to learn more about the men in the 199th Light Infantry Brigade. At night, while cooking their C-rations over smokeless heat tablets, the young draftees would open up and talk about themselves. The Protestant chaplain had gone on the last operation. Now it was the turn of the Catholic chaplain, Father Angelo Liteky, a 37-year-old native of Washington, D.C.

As the patrol snaked along through the jungle, Father Liteky walked in the center of the column alongside company commander Captain Bruce Drees. Suddenly, three khaki-clad Vietnamese ran across an opening less than 100 meters in front of the patrol, disappearing into a nearby clump of woods.

An eerie quiet followed, broken only by the occasional sound of a twig snapping.

Then . . .

Rockets shook the ground. Claymore mines spewed out thousands of pieces of steel. Machine guns chewed up the trees.

Hugging the ground, Father Liteky moved into the tree line to check on the wounded.

A young medic named McElroy was sitting against a tree with his leg blown off.

"Did you say a prayer for me, Padre?" he asked with a strange smile on his face.

"Of course I did . . . you'll be all right. You'll make it."

Shrapnel filled the air all around the chaplain, hitting him in the neck and foot. Still the wounded priest continued to tend the wounded, carrying more than 20 men to a helicopter landing zone for evacuation.

When a blast blew a three-man machine gun crew into the air, he picked up an M-16 rifle from a dead soldier and cradled it under his arms like a G.I. He was thinking he would defend himself if it came down to that.

"I thought if I were going to die, it would be now . . . " But he had second thoughts.

"I thought this would be a hell of a way for a priest to go, so I got rid of it . . . "

He put the rifle aside and crawled to where the three badly wounded men

With three handsets close at hand and a loudspeaker at his elbow, a field phone operator with the U.S. 173rd Airborne catches up on some much needed rest on the crest of Hill 875 near Dak To.

were lying to help them to the evacuation helicopter.

For his actions, Father Liteky received the Medal of Honor. He was the first armed forces chaplain to receive this highest military award for Vietnam service and the fifth to receive it since it was first presented during the Civil War.

While the Viet Cong ambushed smaller American patrols, their North Vietnamese allies drew large American forces away from the population centers and sucked them into remote regions in a stalemate, a war of attrition, first just below the demilitarized zone, then in the hills of Dak To in the Central Highlands.

American paratroopers of the 173rd

Airborne Brigade and infantrymen from the 4th Infantry Division battled four North Vietnamese regiments for 22 days for the hilltop positions, which towered thousands of feet above the Dak To Valley.

At Hill 1338, Captain Donald Scher, 27, of Huntington Station, New York, had hung on for two days, his company driven back by heavy North Vietnamese fire, its food and ammunition supplies depleted.

It was approaching sunset when he sent an urgent radio message to Lieutenant Colonel Jamie Hendrix, of Metter, Georgia, commander of the 3rd Battalion, 12th Regiment, 4th Infantry Division.

"We are low on people, with no food,

no nothing to stay the night."

The order from Hendrix came back: "I don't want you to pull back off the hill unless you're kicked off."

The next morning, Scher's company began another attempt to take the 4,000-foot peak.

In late afternoon, Hendrix radioed again.

"If you have to come off the hill, it will mean starting it all over again tomorrow, like what we've been through today."

"I understand the importance of getting up there," Scher replied. "We'll attack as soon as this last napalm run comes in."

As the hours wore on, Hendrix got on the radio again.

"We're running out of daylight. The sooner we get on top of this thing, the better off we'll all be."

"We are going over the top," Scher radioed back. "We are taking our chances, but we are moving. We are clearing the area with grenades, we're moving up. We are near the top. We still have snipers but we might make it this time."

Seconds later:

"Real light contact. We're moving inch by inch right over the charred place where the bombs hit. Oh, boy! They charred it up good...."

Finally:

"We're over! We've just about got the top cleared. Looks like a battalion was entrenched here. There are eight to ten bodies in the bunkers, five behind me, three on the left, three on the right...."

"We have occupied it all. Snipers are in the trees, but we're shooting them out...."

"Bring in the litters for the wounded, bring in the resupply...."

"We're here to stay!"

Two days later, the 173rd Airborne assaulted the lone holdout, Hill 875 on the southern flank.

The North Vietnamese surrounded two companies on the slopes, raking them with fire so withering that helicopters were unable to get through to lift out more than 100 wounded men. Some had lain on the hillside for 50 hours before a relief force broke through and cleared a landing zone.

The battle for Hill 875 raged for four days.

Then at 11:30 a.m., Thanksgiving Day, two companies from the 4th Division and one company of paratroopers made the final assault and surprisingly met only light resistance. Within 30 minutes they were consolidating their positions on the summit and along the ridge.

The battle of Dak To was over, but at a heavy cost. Two hundred eighty-seven Americans were killed, and more than 1,000 were wounded. The 350-

Denuded of vegetation by the constant bombardment by U.S. planes and artillery, the top of Hill 875 shows the scars of the 21 day battle. 287 Americans lost their lives in the fierce struggle for the hill.

man 2nd Battalion of the 173rd alone suffered 253 casualties. It was left with less than 100 men who were unhurt. The U.S. Military Command claimed more than 1,600 North Vietnamese troops were killed.

"I have always preached a lot about hell," said Major Roy Peters, chaplain of the 173rd Airborne, "but I had never seen it until the last three days."

Such heavy casualties contributed to the more than 15,000 American dead and nearly 100,000 wounded by the end of 1967.

As the war's toll and fury mounted, General Westmoreland came home on a visit to report, "I have never been more encouraged in my four years in Vietnam. . . . We have reached an important point when the end begins to come into view."

Right: *Two youngsters from Dak To village react with shock and hysteria as they view the bodies of dead VC killed by GVN troops during a sweep through the village in July, 1965.*

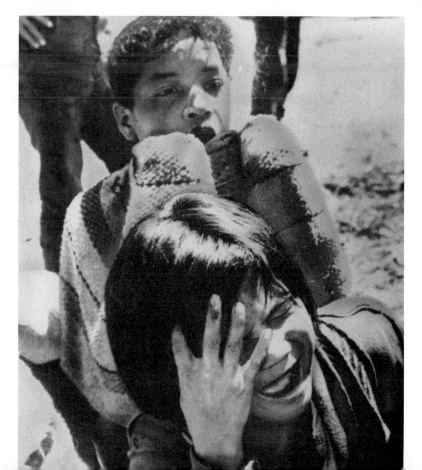

99

CHAPTER 8
THE TURNING POINT

Superstition had it that the Year of the Monkey was a harbinger of bad luck.

Just the same, a mood of festivity prevailed among the Vietnamese for the lunar New Year 1968. It was a time of family reunion, feasting and fireworks. Matched pairs of watermelons were placed on family altars for good luck and in honor of ancestors.

Not so for the military, where the mood was uneasy. The United States was concerned about a threatening concentration of North Vietnamese forces in the Khe Sanh area and other northern regions of South Vietnam. General Westmoreland shifted thousands of American troops into the northern I Military Corps to beef up defenses. Just after it had begun, a 36-hour unilateral truce was canceled by the United States, even as the Viet Cong proclaimed their own cease-fire of seven days for the lunar New Year.

The South Vietnamese canceled holiday furloughs for some of their troops in the northern and central parts of the country. Still, nearly half the army and the national police remained on leave.

The U.S. command put out an alert:

"There may be Viet Cong activities aimed at various United States and Vietnamese headquarters and government billets during the Tet New Year holidays. Viet Cong artillery units and Viet Cong suicide cadres are infiltrating into the capital area."

General Westmoreland had warned of "a resurgence of enemy initiative just before or after Tet, January 30." During a truce for the Gregorian calendar New Year, January 1, the North Vietnamese and Viet Cong shelled more than 40 provincial and district capitals. Infantry troops attacked and occupied some of the capitals briefly. In the Central Highlands, guerrillas overran the town of Tuy Phuoc, considered to be a showcase of Revolutionary Development, the program to rid the countryside of Viet Cong.

As the holidays continued, thousands of visitors from the countryside poured into Saigon by foot, bicycle, bus, scooter and sampan. Most traveled to visit friends and relatives. Many others, however, came for a more violent, sinister purpose. Hidden among the thousands of travelers were hundreds of communist agents and troops. Once in the city, they faded into the population, staying at preselected "safe" houses.

At the pagodas and churches, mock funerals were staged. Inside the coffins, instead of bodies, weapons and ammunition were packed and buried, ready to be dug up from the city's cemeteries when the time came.

Shortly after midnight on January 31, furtive figures disguised as civilians moved in the shadows of Saigon. Exhausted by the Tet celebrations, the city took little notice. Even though there had been a rash of attacks elsewhere in Vietnam the previous day, the midnight-to-dawn curfew had been suspended. In the pre-dawn hours, some 4,500 Viet Cong gathered in the cemeteries and other designated points to pick up their weapons. The guerrillas fastened the top buttons of their white shirts or slipped red armbands onto their sleeves to identify themselves to other Viet Cong. That time had come.

Attack on the Embassy

At an auto repair shop in downtown Saigon, 23 Viet Cong sappers assembled. They were members of the elite Viet Cong C-10 Sapper Battalion, all native Saigonese. Picking up antitank rockets, automatic weapons, satchel charges and demolitions, they

---

Facing page: *Members of the 2nd Battalion of the 3rd Regiment, ARVN 1st Division peer cautiously through a gate of the Imperial Palace in the citadel at Hue.* Above: *Aerial view of the U.S. Embassy in Saigon.*

U.S. troops look out from behind sandbags on the roof of the U.S. Embassy on February 2. Fighting raged through the streets of the South Vietnamese capital for nearly two weeks after the attack on the embassy.

drove to the U.S. Embassy along tree-lined Thong Nhut Boulevard.

Allan Wendt, an economic-commercial officer at the embassy, had the duty that night. He was asleep in room 433, the duty officer's quarters on the fourth floor. Just before 3:00 a.m., an antitank rocket blasted a hole in the outer wall of the four-acre compound, shaking even the newly constructed six-story building.

The explosion jolted Wendt from his sleep. Rolling out of bed, he reached for the telephone and called John Calhoun, a political officer at the embassy. "As I was speaking, another explosion tore into the building.... I crawled under the bed while talking to Mr. Calhoun and emerged from under the bed just as [James] Griffin, who was on duty in communications, came in and asked what was happening. I said I was not sure but I presumed the embassy was being attacked. I quickly dressed, gathered up my few personal possessions, and withdrew into the communications room next door, which was safer than the duty room and had more telephones."

Outside, the squad of sappers crawled one by one through the hole in the wall surrounding the embassy compound. They carried with them satchel charges and demolitions to penetrate the embassy building.

Wendt heard the rattle of automatic weapons fire, then more explosions. The fire seemed so close to him that he thought he might not make it through the night.

"We feared not only that penetration of the embassy was inevitable but that

our lives were in imminent danger."

To find out what was happening in the embassy compound below, Wendt called down to the Marine guard in the embassy's lobby, Sergeant Ronald Harper, even though he thought the guard might already be dead. To Wendt's surprise, Harper answered. This would be the first of many conversations Wendt would have with Harper, who for the next six hours would remain virtually the only source of information on what was happening in the compound.

"Harper told us the VC were inside the compound but not in the embassy building itself. He said he could hear them talking outside the building. He did not know how many of them there were."

A few minutes later, Harper phoned Wendt telling him that there was a wounded Marine on the first floor, and he asked Griffin and him to come and take the soldier to safety. Wendt, somewhat apprehensive, went downstairs in the elevator.

"With the aid of Sergeant Harper, I picked up the wounded Marine and put him on the elevator. Griffin then came down and helped me assist him to the fourth floor. Then, and always thereafter, we locked the elevators in place so that they could not be called down to the ground floor had the VC gotten into the building."

A hurried and fearful glance at the ground floor revealed that considerable damage had already been done.

"We carried the wounded man into the fourth floor duty room and placed him on the bed I had been sleeping in.

He was covered with blood but did not appear to be critically wounded. His leg seemed broken and he was obviously suffering from shock. Unfortunately, none of us had any usable knowledge of first aid, and there was little we could do for him. He kept asking for a corpsman.

"We tried to call the 17th field hospital but could not get through. We gave the wounded man some water and two Bufferin tablets, and I took his .38-caliber revolver. It was the only weapon I had and I was to carry it with me for the next five and a half hours...."

Told that the medevac and ammunition choppers were on their way, Wendt and Griffin carried the Marine to the roof of the embassy, where the landing pad was located. It would be another 45 minutes before the first helicopter arrived to evacuate him and two other wounded Americans.

Washington was stunned by the magnitude and boldness of the Tet offensive. Only a few months earlier, General Westmoreland had been saying he could see light at the end of the tunnel. Now they were being told that the embassy was under attack, along with a growing number of towns and U.S. installations.

President Johnson kept in close touch with Ambassador Ellsworth Bunker, who was moved from his home to a safe location, and with General Westmoreland. Throughout the day the President would receive nearly 25 cables from Saigon.

The White House situation room buzzed with activity. At 5:00 a.m., Philip Habib, the deputy assistant secretary of state, telephoned Wendt to find out what was happening. Wendt reported the Viet Cong had surrounded the embassy and that U.S. military policemen and Vietnamese police had surrounded the compound but had not yet made a move inside. Wendt also told Habib a reaction force had been promised, but two hours after the attack none had arrived.

While Wendt continued his vigil in the embassy's communications room, another drama was unfolding in a two-story, white frame house on the embassy grounds. George Jacobson, a 56-year-old senior American diplomat from Hutchinson, Minnesota, was trapped in the upstairs room of the house. From his window, he had watched the early stages of the attack. Now the battle had reached his house.

Private First Class Paul Healey and a Marine guard dashed into the ground floor of Jacobson's house to check on him. A shadowy figure emerged from the toilet. At first, Healey thought it was Jacobson. He quickly found out it wasn't.

Two shots rang out from an M-16

rifle that the Viet Cong guerrilla had picked up from a dead American. They missed Healey and the Marine guard. Healey threw two grenades at the guerrilla, wounding him. The Viet Cong got off another burst of fire, this time wounding the Marine.

"We immediately called Sergeant Harper and told him of this plan. He pleaded with us to stop the use of gas, since by this time, about 7:30, the U.S. MPs had fought their way into the compound. We would be gassing our own men. I called Major Hudson back at once. After a fifteen-minute delay, he said the gas probably would be used anyway. At one point, he said not to worry, that the cavalry was coming. I had heard so much about the air cavalry that I thought he was being serious...."

As two companies of American military policemen fought their way into the embassy compound at daybreak, a dozen helicopters swooped in over downtown Saigon and landed heavily armed paratroopers on the rooftop. Heading up to the roof to see if the rescue helicopters had landed, Wendt ran into the paratroopers.

"As I stepped off the elevator on the sixth floor, I was greeted by a strange sight. Standing before me were five paratroopers in full battle dress from the 101st Airborne Division. They carried M-16s, M-79 grenade launchers, hand grenades, and knives. I asked for the platoon commander. Major (Hillel) Schwartz stepped forward, and I told him I was the duty officer. He offered me a grenade, which I declined. He said thirty more men would land soon."

Wendt told Major Schwartz that he knew of no Viet Cong in the building. Just the same, Schwartz was taking no chances. He deployed his men to secure the building floor by floor, beginning with the sixth. By 8:55 a.m., the American forces had regained control of the compound.

By now, General Westmoreland had arrived. He summoned Wendt to the Marine guard's office and advised him that the building should be cleaned up as soon as possible and the staff be at work by noon. At Westmoreland's request, Wendt returned to the fourth floor and put through a flash call to Philip Habib, telling him that the embassy had been secured.

The military police decided to use tear gas to root the sapper out and threw a gas mask up to Jacobson on the second floor. They also tossed him a .45-caliber pistol. To this point, Jacobson had been armed with only a grenade, which he had been saving for such a moment. He had just begun pulling the gas mask over his face when the Viet Cong soldier staggered up on the landing.

For a moment, the two just faced each other, the middle-aged American diplomat and the young Vietnamese guerrilla. The bleeding guerrilla reacted first, firing three shots. Jacobson fired two back and the Viet Cong soldier fell mortally wounded.

In the embassy building, Wendt and the others uneasily waited out the siege.

"... The atmosphere in the code room was one of generally unrelieved tension mixed with frustration and helplessness," said Wendt. "Sometimes the tension would ease, but periodically, another rocket round would hit the wall to remind us of our plight. There were lulls in the firing, but they never lasted long."

Several times, Wendt checked the embassy's rooftop helipad, but there was still no sign of the promised relief forces. Eventually, he telephoned the U.S. Military Command operations center and pleaded with a Major Hudson "somewhat despairingly for relief from the ground."

"Finally, he said a mechanized infantry unit with heavy armor was on its way," said Wendt. "We asked how long it would take. He said the unit was on the outskirts of the city and moving slowly. It never arrived."

"Between 6:30 and 7:00, Major Hudson called to say that there could be no [rooftop helicopter] landing before daylight because of poor visibility, despite the roof lights being on. Eventually, dawn broke. Major Hudson said the situation had become critical. We readily agreed. He said the latest plan was to gas the VC inside the compound and then land troops on the roof. The gas choppers were to be sent right away.

A detail of three Marines raised the Stars and Stripes in front of the scarred building at 11:45 a.m., nearly five hours later than the normal flag-raising time. The Great Seal of the United States had been dislodged from the wall above the embassy entrance by bullets. The lower floor of the embassy building was littered with debris. Four gaping holes were left in the front wall. The bodies of two Viet Cong lay a few yards from one of the holes.

"In summary," Westmoreland said, "the enemy's well-laid plan went afoul. There was some superficial damage. The enemy deceitfully has taken advantage of the Tet truce in order to create maximum consternation in South Vietnam, particularly in populated areas. In my opinion, this is a diversionary effort to take the attention away from the northern part of the country."

All across South Vietnam, coordinated attacks were under way from the demilitarized zone (DMZ) to the Mekong Delta in the biggest offensive of the war.

Seventy thousand North Vietnamese and Viet Cong troops struck at more than three-fourths of South Vietnam's 44 provincial capitals, at 64 district towns, scores of villages and a dozen American bases.

But the most spectacular action was in the capital of Saigon.

Three American military police kneel behind a wall at the entrance to the U.S. consulate next to the U.S. Embassy. In the foreground lie the bodies of two Americans killed in earlier fighting.

Top: *The Central Market Hall of the provincial capital of Ben Tre.* Bottom: *Vietnamese Marines train their rifles on VC positions in a residential section of Saigon.*

Top: *Specialist 4 Gerald Bolden of Fairfield, California, carries a pregnant Vietnamese woman to an evacuation helicopter. The woman went into labor as she was evacuated from her village. The child was born en route to the hospital.* Bottom: *U.S. military policemen dash through sniper fire in an alley in Saigon.*

War Comes to Saigon

Saigon turned into a battleground.

House-to-house fighting erupted, particularly in Cholon, the Chinese section of Saigon. Bombs and rockets reduced some neighborhoods to charred ruins. The city shut down, and at one point, the only shops open were those of the coffin makers.

An armored squadron of the U.S. 25th Infantry Division rushed from its base in Cu Chi, 25 miles away, to drive back the Viet Cong from Tan Son Nhut Airport. When Vietnamese paratroopers were unable to drive guerrillas from the government radio station, they set the building on fire. Then they cut down the Viet Cong soldiers as they fled the burning building.

A running battle flared across the fairways of the golf course. No place was safe or sacred. At the old French na-

tional cemetery, fighting raged where many heroes of Vietnam's wars were buried.

The Viet Cong went from door to door telling people, "We have come to liberate Saigon." Their liberation had a bloody edge to it. They beheaded the commander of a South Vietnamese training school in his home and blew up his wife and five of their six children with grenades. They executed civilians caught with South Vietnamese flags in their possession.

The South Vietnamese would have their revenge, an eye for an eye.

Eddie Adams of the Associated Press was with an NBC-TV crew near the An Ouang Pagoda in Cholon, where the Viet Cong set up a command post. Adams was photographing South Vietnamese forces trying to fight their way into the pagoda. In a few minutes, he would capture on film an image that

would shock the world.

"As the fighting died down," Adams said, "we started to walk to our car, parked two blocks away. In front of us, the Vietnamese police had just captured a Viet Cong lieutenant minutes after he killed a policeman. I followed them, and we got to a street corner. There, General Nguyen Ngoc Loan [chief of the national police] walked over and shot him in the head. Then he turned to us and said, 'They killed many of my men —and many of yours.'"

Adams caught the instant of execution as General Loan pulled the trigger of the revolver held to the prisoner's head. The man grimaced in agony and fell to the ground, blood spurting from the side of his head. Adams' picture was a brutal snapshot of a brutal war. More than any war story, it brought home to Americans the ugliness of the war being fought in Vietnam.

Top: *U.S. helicopter rakes a VC position with a rocket fire in a village opposite U.S. installation at Khu Gia Vien.* Middle: *Black smoke from a napalm strike rises behind a Buddhist pagoda in Saigon.* Bottom: *General Nguyen Ngoc Loan executes a VC suspect. The photo by AP photographer Eddie Adams shocked the world and earned a Pulitzer Prize in 1969.*

Top: *U.S. soldiers view the bodies of Viet Cong guerrillas killed during an attack on the Central Highland capital of Pleiku.* Bottom: *Smoke pours from a building in Cholon, the Chinese section of Saigon. Much of that "city within a city" was destroyed during the Tet attacks.*

Top left: *May, 1968. Civilians search through the debris of their homes destroyed by communist rockets landing in the heart of Saigon.* Top right: *Rescue workers search through the rubble of the U.S.–South Vietnamese television compound in Saigon for survivors of communist bombing. Three Vietnamese were killed and thirty others injured by the blast.* Bottom: *Wounded soldiers patiently await medical treatment outside makeshift medical facilities.*

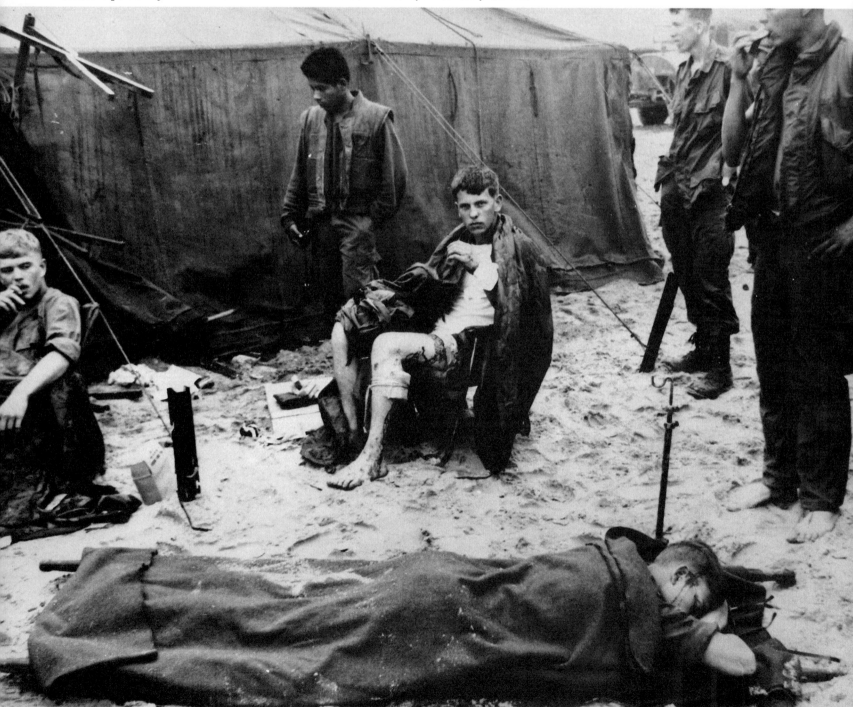

The war had caused disruptions before in the South Vietnamese capital, but now the city's three million people were face to face with it. Bodies lay in the streets. Hundreds of civilians were killed, caught in the crossfire.

A wealthy Chinese importer ignored the stop-whistle of a nervous American MP at a Saigon intersection. He was killed.

Doyle Clark, 33, of Covina, California, and Billy Stein, of Sacramento, California, both entomologists employed by Pacific Architects and Engineering, tried to flee in their jeep when fighting broke out near their home beside the Saigon golf course. They were killed 30 yards from their gate. Mike Mealey, a neighbor from California, survived by taking cover under his bed for 29 hours. In his house in one of Saigon's suburbs, Richard Taylor, of Auburn, Maine, clutched an unfamiliar weapon to his breast. A missionary with the Christian Missionary Alliance, the last thing he wanted was to take up arms. However, as he pointed out, "We have no choice. We have bullet holes in our shutters."

Thousands more civilians were wounded or became refugees, carrying their children through the streets in search of food and shelter. Hospitals were jammed with the wounded, with at least two in every bed.

Tom Durant, a civilian doctor from Boston who was in Saigon to help the South Vietnamese medical corps, said there were so many casualties that a big enough blood bank was not available.

"The Cho Rai Hospital was cut off because it was in Cholon," Durant said. "Cho Rai is the biggest hospital in Saigon. And there was no communication between hospitals except by telephone, which was practically impossible. So you

had people, ambulances going through, cutting through firing lines and getting shot at. It was total chaos and that was probably the major problem.

"We had Pat Burns, also a volunteer worker here, who went to the hotel that she was staying in and got all the American civilians who were living in that hotel. And we sent an Army truck to pick them up and bring them to Saigon Hospital along with whatever orange juice and Jack Daniels we could have to give them something for donating their blood.

"Already we had about four hundred wounded that day. Cho Rai Hospital became totally functionless because twenty thousand refugees moved in. We felt that was the most protective place they could be, so it was wall-to-wall refugees. They were in the operating room, they were everywhere. It was a crazy place."

Helping wounded comrades.

107

Smoke from a napalm air strike rises over the Imperial City as houseboats glide serenely down the Perfume River toward the center of Hue.

The Tragedy of Hue

By Sunday, February 4, order had been restored in much of the country. U.S. officials said the North Vietnamese and Viet Cong did not hold any objective of military importance and that they were being pushed out of a few areas they still occupied.

One of these was Hue, the ancient imperial capital of Vietnam, established more than 200 years before Christ and the seat of the Old Annam empire for 21 centuries. It was here that the North Vietnamese chose to launch their most ambitious effort. On January 30, six thousand regulars of North Vietnam's 4th, 5th, and 6th Regiments marched four abreast in parade formation across the canal bridges on the city's southern outskirts.

With each company was a commissar who wore a gold Ho Chi Minh button and carried dossiers on people marked for arrest or execution. Their bloody role during the communist occupation would not be revealed until the end of the siege.

On the morning of January 31, as news of an attack on Hue reached the U.S. base at Phu Bai, eight miles to the south, first one and then a second company from the 1st Battalion, 1st Marine

Above: *Dug in behind columns of the old Imperial Palace, South Vietnamese Marines look over the palace courtyard on February 16.* Left: *Supported by a tank, U.S. Marines fire down a street near the citadel in Hue.*

Regiment advanced toward the ancient capital. Along the way to the city, the reaction force added four tanks headed for the DMZ.

The members of one squad from Foxtrot Company paid a heavy price in the street fighting that followed. Advancing up a street trying to locate any U.S. citizens cut off during the fighting, the Marines came under heavy fire. "That

day we were in the lead," recalled 19-year-old Marine Private John Moore, a machine gunner from Orlando, Florida. "I dove over a wall after crossing the street a couple of times. Cement chips and branches flew everywhere. It was so bad we couldn't even pop up and fire."

Behind Moore, his fellow squad members scattered to avoid the deadly hail of bullets. They lay there unable to fight back. "You never really see them," said Corporal Paul Hamilton, 21, of Boston. "Every now and then there is a gun barrel in a window [but] we couldn't see to hit the window. Fire came from everywhere."

"Their fire ricocheted off the walls and streets," recalled Lance Corporal Nick Lendino, 18, of Massapequa, New York. "We were just praying at the time."

Finally a tank rolled up the street to support the pinned down Marines. Buttoned up inside against the communist fire, however, the tank crew could not hear the shouts of Moore and Lendino telling them where the communists were hidden.

While the tank fired blindly down the street, Moore ran behind it, picking up the bodies of two Marines lying in the street. As he lifted them onto the tank, a VC rocket slammed into the armored vehicle, throwing the dead Marines back onto the street. Moore then picked them up a second time and dragged them out of the line of fire.

South Vietnamese soldiers and shop owners move through the rubble clogging the main street in Hue. Much of the city, the center of higher learning and religion in South Vietnam, was destroyed during the fight.

Finally, as support arrived, the squad resumed its advance up the street. They had paid dearly for the ground. In one 150-yard stretch, they had lost five dead and nine more had been wounded. Early that afternoon, they finally reached their destination, the MACV compound. It had taken them six hours to travel the eight-plus miles from Phu Bai to the compound.

The bloody experience of the squad of Marines from Foxtrot Company foreshadowed what was to come in the 24-day battle for the city. Fighting from house to house, the Marines paid dearly for every yard. Recalling another urban battle fought by U.S. Marines, one U.S. commander at Hue offered, "Seoul was tough, but this—well, it's something else." When it was over, most Marines welcomed the return to the countryside.

It took the equivalent of nearly two divisions of South Vietnamese and American troops to recapture Hue. In the process, much of the city had been leveled; some officials estimated nearly 70 percent of the homes and many historical treasures of the past had been destroyed. The human toll had been tremendous. U.S. officials reported 142 U.S. Marines killed along with 384 South Vietnamese. North Vietnamese losses were estimated at 8,000 dead.

An even more gruesome fate had been meted out to the civilians of Hue. In a massive political purge, the communists executed more than 2,800 of the city's residents. Some were shot. Many others were buried alive. The victims included civil servants, teachers, government officials, military personnel, priests and any men who appeared to be of military age. It was a singularly brutal incident in the growing list of tragedies that marked the history of the Vietnam war.

U.S. Marines reach up to grasp a wounded comrade as he is lowered from a rooftop in Hue. The U.S. 1st Marines earned a presidential unit citation for its actions at Hue, and Hue was added to the battle streamers of the Marine Corps.

The message on his flak jacket sums up this Marine's feelings about Khe Sanh. More than 200 Marines lost their lives at Khe Sanh.

Above: *U.S. Marines push toward Khe Sanh along Highway 9 on April 4 during Operation Pegasus. Pegasus, which began on April 1, finally relieved the forces at Khe Sanh on April 15.* Below: *Smoke from a North Vietnamese rocket and mortar attack hangs over section of U.S. position at Khe Sanh.*

Khe Sanh

As the Marines fought and died on the streets of Hue, other Marines, some 60 miles to the northwest at Khe Sanh, waged a much different battle. Theirs was a battle of patience, raw nerves and isolation; of rats, mud and rain; of waiting. They had no ground to gain, no area to clean out. They were told to hold, just hold.

General Westmoreland felt that the base at Khe Sanh was an important "cork" in the enemy's infiltration pipeline. Without it, he reasoned, the NVA would simply sweep into the valley of Quang Tri and across the Cam Lo River, pushing all the way to the sea, 30 miles to the east.

The siege began in early January. Heavy NVA artillery started a bombardment of the camp that would continue nonstop for the next three months. On the average, 150 rounds of artillery, rockets and mortars pounded the base and its 5,500-Marine garrison (from the 9th Marines, 3rd Marine Division, and the 26th Marines, 5th Marine Division, which was detached to the 3rd Marine Division during Khe Sanh) each day. On some days the bombardment reached more than 1,000 rounds. Associated Press correspondent John T. Wheeler told of the misery of the defenders in this dispatch filed from Khe Sanh, February 12:

The first shell burst caught the Marines outside the bunkers filling sandbags. More exploding rockets sent showers of hot fragments zinging. The Americans dove for cover.
"Corpsman! Corpsman!"
The shout came from off to the right.
"We've got wounded here!"
"Corpsman! Corpsman!"
The shouts now came from the distance. You could see the men dragging a bleeding buddy toward cover.

Inside the bunkers, the Marines hugged their legs and bowed their heads, unconsciously trying to make themselves as small as possible. The tempo of the shelling increased and the small opening to the bunker seemed in their minds to grow to the size of a barn door. The 6,000 sandbags around and over the bunker seemed wafer thin. Although it could increase their chances of survival only minutely, men shifted their positions to get closer to the ground. Some measured the angle of the doorway and tried to wiggle a bit more behind those next to them. There were no prayers uttered aloud. Two men growled a stream of profanity at the North Vietnamese gunners who might snuff out their lives at any moment. Near misses rocked the bunker and sent dirt cascading down everyone's neck.

Outside, the random explosions sent thousands of pounds of shrapnel tearing into sandbags and battering already damaged mess halls and tent areas long ago destroyed and abandoned for a life of fear and filth underground.

This is life in the V Ring, a sharpshooter's

U.S. Marine climbs atop sandbags protecting a hut near helicopter landing strip at Khe Sanh.

Above: *Marines deepen trenches, which resemble the trenches of the First World War, at Khe Sanh.* Below: *White phosphorous bombs create a psychedelic smoke screen for a supply plane landing at Khe Sanh.*

term for the inner part of the bull's eye. At Khe Sanh, the V Ring for the North Vietnamese gunners neatly covers the bunkers of Bravo Company, 3rd Reconnaissance Battalion. In three weeks, more than half the company had been killed or wounded. It was a recon's bad luck to live in an area bordered by an ammunition dump, a flight-line loading area and the 26th Marine Regiment's command post.

Shrapnel and shell holes cover the area. The incoming rounds could hardly be noticed once the barrage stopped, such is the desolation. And then the shells did stop. Silent men turned their faces from one to the other. Several men scrambled out of the bunker to see if more dead or wounded men from their unit were outside. Medics scurried through the area, crouching low.

Inside one bunker, a Marine returned to his paperback book, a tale of Wild West adventure. Another man whose hand had

A young Marine curls up in his trench with a book.

stopped in the midst of strumming a guitar resumed playing. Two men in a card game began flipping the soggy pasteboards again.

The shelling wasn't worth discussing. It was too commonplace and none from Bravo Company had been hit this time. Like jungle rot, snipers and rats, artillery fire was something to be hated and accepted at the same time. But the shellfire had taken its toll. Minutes before the barrage opened, Army Specialist 4 William Hankinson had drifted off from other members of his communications team assigned to this Marine base. When the first shell hit, he dived into a Marine bunker. After the explosions stopped, he talked with the Marines awhile before starting back to his bunker.

A white-faced leatherneck joined the group.

"You look kind of sick," a Marine buddy said. "What happened?"

"The whole Army bunker got wiped out," he replied. "Jesus, what a mess."

Hankinson started to run toward the smashed bunker where his friends' shattered bodies lay. Marines caught and blocked him. Then with a tenderness not at all out of place for hardened fighting men, they began to console the Army specialist, a man most had never spoken to before that day....

Carrying an M-60 machine gun, a U.S. Marine climbs a hill near Khe Sanh late in April.

The 77-day siege of Khe Sanh ended on April 5 when a relief column of 12,000 American and South Vietnamese soldiers reached the battered base. The North Vietnamese had withdrawn, fading back into the jungle; what had been billed as the showdown battle of the war never materialized.

U.S. officers said the heavy air strikes kept the North Vietnamese from launching an assault (American planes dropped nearly 100,000 tons of explosives around Khe Sanh, one-sixth of the total tonnage dropped by U.S. planes during the entire three years of Korea). Still, the cost of holding the base had been high. More than 200 Marines lost their lives at Khe Sanh, and another 1,600 were wounded, one-third of the entire garrison. U.S. intelligence officers estimated that the North Vietnamese lost more than 3,000 troops.

Sergeant Edward Pelletrier of the 26th Marines neatly summed up the feelings of those who served at Khe Sanh: "I was glad to leave and I never want to go back."

The Legacy of Tet

The Tet offensive produced some disturbing revelations. It underscored the vulnerability of South Vietnam's cities, once considered safe. In the first two weeks of fighting, South Vietnam and its allies lost 4,583 troops, of which 1,113 were Americans. The United States and Saigon commands reported more than 30,000 North Vietnamese soldiers were killed.

Tet also raised questions about strategy and tactics, including the effectiveness of search-and-destroy operations. U.S. officials also said there was a need for the South Vietnamese to take on more of the fighting.

Most important, however, was the domestic reaction to Tet. Around the country, antiwar protesters staged hundreds of demonstrations, and in Washington, congressional opposition to the war reached a new high. Finally, on Sunday night, March 31, President Johnson addressed the nation:

"We are prepared to move immediately toward peace through negotiations.... So tonight, in the hope that this action will lead to early talks, I am taking the first step to de-escalate the conflict. We are reducing—substantially reducing—the present level of hostilities, and we are doing so unilaterally

March 31, 1968. President Johnson tells a shocked nation that "I shall not seek, and I will not accept, the nomination for another term as president."

and at once. Tonight I have ordered our aircraft and our naval vessels to make no attacks on North Vietnam except in the area north of the demilitarized zone where the continuing enemy buildup threatens allied forward positions and where the movements of their troops and supplies are clearly related to that threat. The area in which we are stopping our attacks includes almost ninety percent of North Vietnam's population and most of its territory.... Now, as in the past, the United States is ready to send its representatives to any forum, at any time, to discuss the means of bringing this ugly war to an end.... I call upon President Ho Chi Minh to respond positively, and favorably, to this new step toward peace."

Then, Johnson concluded with a startling statement that was not in his prepared text:

"I shall not seek, and I will not accept,

Left behind by his comrades, a wounded North Vietnamese soldier was captured by U.S. Marines near Hill 881 near Khe Sanh.

the nomination of my party for another term as your president." Vietnam had claimed yet another victim.

Brigadier General Douglas Kinnard, a West Point graduate who served two tours of duty in Vietnam, said in his book, *The War Managers,* that Tet was the turning point of the war.

London newspapers herald the surprising news of Johnson's decision not to seek reelection. A tireless worker and shrewd politician, Johnson finally succumbed to the problem that had plagued his administration from the start.

"The Tet offensive, as is well known," he wrote, "was the watershed of the Second Indochinese War: a United States–GVN (Government of Vietnam) military victory in Vietnam, but a tremendous psychological defeat in the United States which brought down the Johnson Administration. The Johnson decision to restrict bombing in the North and to withdraw from the 1968 presidential election led the North Vietnamese to the conference table in Paris—and to a change in United States objectives. In brief, a limit to the United States commitment of forces was established, and the South Vietnamese were put on notice that in the future they would be expected to do more in their own defense....

"It was clear after Tet 1968 that the United States could not destroy the enemy forces or force them completely from South Vietnam. Not everyone drew this conclusion immediately. To some in the military, Tet seemed an opportunity to mobilize the United States society and secure a military victory. By the civilian bureaucracy, however, Tet was read as a failure of policy which pointed up the need of the nation to get itself out of the Vietnamese quagmire as soon as possible."

Above: *A Chicago policeman charges demonstrators in Chicago's Lincoln Park during the Democratic Convention in August, 1968.* Below: *Demonstrators use park benches to construct a barricade in Grant Park near the Conrad Hilton, headquarters for the Democratic Convention.*

CHAPTER 9
GOING HOME

While the United States and North Vietnamese talked peace in the spring of 1968, they launched new operations of war.

On the first day American bombing was curtailed below the 20th parallel, U.S. planes flew more than 100 missions over the southern portion of North Vietnam. On April 7, the total rose to 134, the highest number in three months.

In the A Shau Valley, U.S. 1st Air Cavalry troops launched a major drive where intelligence showed that the North Vietnamese 325C Division had taken haven in retreat from Khe Sanh, 50 miles to the northwest.

And in the heaviest fighting since the Tet offensive, the U.S. 3rd Marine Division battled North Vietnamese troops around Dong Ha and Quang Tri just below the DMZ.

On April 3, the Hanoi government announced its willingness to open peace talks. Rather than leading to a lessening of hostilities, however, the agreement marked an upsurge in communist attacks. "Charles [short for Victor Charlie, U.S. troop nickname for the VC] is beginning to get his shit together ever since we heard the rumor of peace talks," wrote Marine Corporal Don Lohnes to his friend Ed Bell on April 7. "About three days ago, Charlie held reveille on us here at Quang Tri. It was about six in the morning on a Sunday, no less. I was sound asleep because we are allowed to sleep a little later on holidays. All of a sudden, like a Phantom jet, the rockets sped in our direction. You talk about being scared. Well, bud, I was one scared sonofa . . . They only hit us with about ten rounds, then the Army opened up with twin 40s and got three of the four positions that Charlie had. Needless to say, I have slept a little on the light side ever since then."

On May 5, eight days before the opening session in the Centre de Conferences Internationale, the North Vietnamese and Viet Cong launched a mini-Tet offensive in efforts to strengthen their bargaining position. More than 100 cities, towns and bases were shelled, and battles raged across six sections of Saigon.

By the end of the offensive, the U.S.

U.S. and North Vietnamese delegations settle in for the first meeting of the peace talks in the International Conference Hall in Paris on May 13, 1968. These peace negotiations would drag on for four long years before a settlement was reached.

115

Above: *June, 1969. Captain Noble, commander of the U.S. Special Forces team at the besieged base at Ben Het watches an ammunition dump burn from behind a sandbag wall.* Below: *A Buddhist monk leads prayers during a ceremony marking the first transferral of a major U.S. Naval base—My Tho in the Mekong Delta—to the South Vietnamese navy.*

command estimated that 5,000 VC and NVA had been killed. American casualties also ran high. In the week ending May 11, 562 U.S. soldiers were killed and nearly 2,000 were killed during the entire month, both new highs for the war.

American casualties now stood at 22,951 dead since January 1, 1961. Between May and December, 8,000 more Americans died while the peace negotiations crawled along inconclusively. North Vietnam demanded an unconditional halt to the bombing of all of its territory before any progress could be made. Finally, in exchange for Hanoi's acceptance of South Vietnam as a negotiating partner of the United States, President Johnson halted the bombing on November 1.

"I have reached this decision . . . in the belief that this action can lead to progress toward a peaceful settlement of the Vietnam War," he said. "What we now expect—what we have a right to expect—are prompt, productive, serious and intensive negotiations in an atmosphere that is conducive to progress."

After three years, eight months and 24 days, the bombing of North Vietnam stopped. In that time, American

116

pilots had flown 100,000 missions and unloaded almost a half million tons of bombs across North Vietnam. More than 900 American planes had been lost and nearly 1,500 airmen had been killed, captured or listed as missing in action.

Nixon and Vietnamization

The term "Vietnamization" was coined by Defense Secretary Melvin Laird. The program was designed to turn the war over to the South Vietnamese—to train them, equip them, and finally leave them to fight the communists while the United States trooped back home.

President Nixon's plan was divided into three stages: In the first stage, the U.S. forces would turn over combat responsibility to the South Vietnamese while continuing to provide air and logistical support. In the second stage, the United States would help the South Vietnamese to develop their own support capabilities through military aid and training; and in the final stage, the United States would restrict itself to a strictly advisory effort. Throughout, U.S. forces in Vietnam would gradually be reduced.

To implement the new policy, Nixon turned to the new MACV commander, General Creighton W. Abrams, who had replaced Westmoreland in 1968. The strategy Abrams adopted shunned the large-scale search-and-destroy operations favored by Westmoreland for smaller, company- and platoon-

General Creighton W. Abrams. Abrams succeeded Westmoreland as head of MACV in 1968.

sized operations. The larger, more offensive operations he left to the South Vietnamese.

As the United States moved toward accomplishing the first stage of Vietnamization, they also began to prepare the South Vietnamese to support their own operations. Millions of dollars were poured into training programs. By the end of 1969, the South Vietnamese armed forces had doubled in size, topping more than 1 million. At the same time, the United States turned over a huge arsenal of weapons and vehicles, including 700,000 M-16 rifles, 600 pieces of artillery, 30,000 grenade launchers, 10,000 machine guns and thousands of vehicles including trucks, tanks, armored personnel carriers, helicopters, planes and jets.

Probably the most rapid progress was made by the U.S. naval forces operating in the Mekong Delta. The brown-water navy that patrolled a vast, intricate network of waterways that crisscrossed the delta was turned over to the Vietnamese. Included in the turnover were 242 U.S. Navy river craft

Members of B Battery, 6th Battalion, 108th U.S. Artillery Group, stand at attention as South Vietnamese soldiers march forward to take command of six 105mm howitzers during a ceremony formally marking the turnover of the equipment in Da Nang in November, 1969.

worth $68 million and two major riverine bases.

Despite the impressive statistical achievements racked up by the Vietnamization program in its first year, many critics doubted it would succeed. They argued that the United States was making an army "graven in our image," requiring funding, equipment

and resources far beyond Vietnam's capabilities. "We live with the military assistance of the United States," said one South Vietnamese general. "Without that aid, our army would die." Regarding the attempts to train a South Vietnamese air force, a U.S. instructor noted that "there is no such thing as a helicopter repair manual in Vietnamese," adding, "I couldn't imagine myself going over there to learn Vietnamese and fly." Captain Paul Kalill, a 29-year-old adviser from Pittsfield, Massachusetts, summed up the plight of the entire Vietnamization effort. "We were taking people who had probably never been more than one mile from the place that they were born and were still taking water out of the kind of vats Christ changed water into wine from two thousand years ago, and trying to bring them into the twentieth century overnight."

Abrams salutes his departing predecessor, General Westmoreland, during a brief farewell ceremony at Tan Son Nhut airbase.

Captain Paul Kalill (right). Although an Army officer, Kalill operated under the control of the State Department as an adviser in government development.

117

Above: *Lieutenant Colonel Edith Knox. Although the nurses serving in Vietnam saw little actual combat, they witnessed the results every day.* Below: *Racing against time. A U.S. medic rushes a Vietnamese soldier, the only survivor of a helicopter crash, to a nearby hospital.*

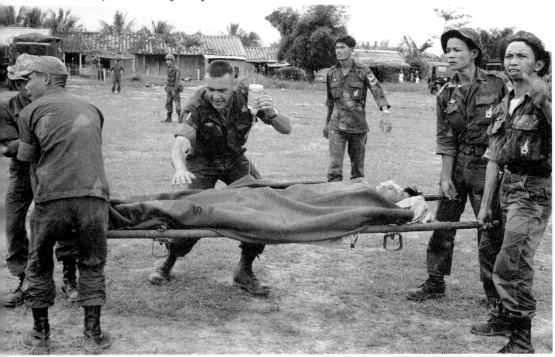

Still the War

While the United States implemented its Vietnamization plan in 1969 and started the process of turning the war over to the South Vietnamese, thousands of Americans died on the battlefield. During 1969 more than 11,500 Americans lost their lives in Vietnam and another 70,000 were wounded.

Lieutenant Colonel Edith Knox, a 42-year-old native of Kilgore, Texas, who was the chief nurse at the 67th Evacuation Hospital in Qui Nhon, wanted to run the first time battlefield casualties were brought in.

"The first time I was there," said Colonel Knox, "maybe a couple of days when I made my first rounds and walked into the receiving and emer-

gency room, just after they had brought in four young men, all with amputated legs. And I just took one look at it and I thought, I'm not sure I can handle this. And I left the room immediately and went outside. And then I thought to myself, No, I'm the chief nurse, and those nurses that are working in there have to handle this every day. And I have to learn to handle it. So then I walked back in. But it's just, I think, that I had never seen anything quite like that. And the first time it really hit me, and I'm sure it did every nurse that was over there.

"I think probably one of the most difficult things for me was when I'd be making rounds and some young man would say to me, 'Colonel, how do I write and tell my wife I don't have a

Above: Corpsman Walter V. Marvin of El Dorado, Arkansas, helps a wounded Marine during the battle for Hill 174. Corpsmen suffered heavy casualties while caring for the wounded on the battlefield. Below: Wounded while charging a communist position, a U.S. sergeant is pulled to safety by his company medic.

U.S. Army nurses Captain Gladys E. Sepulveda (left) of Ponce, Puerto Rico, and Second Lieutenant Lois Ferrari of Pittsburgh, Pennsylvania, rest on some sandbags at Cam Ranh Bay while awaiting transportation to the 8th Field Hospital at Nha Trang.

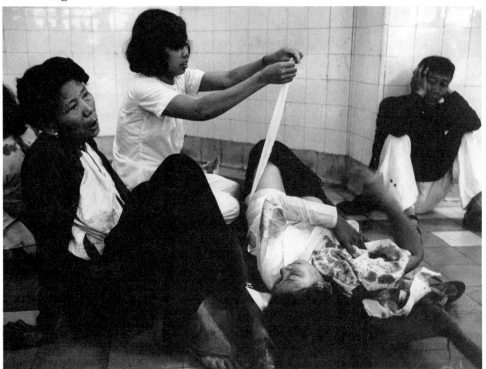

Above: A nurse bandages the leg of a Vietnamese woman wounded during a VC rocket attack on Saigon. Below: Lieutenant Mary Huepers of Alvin, Texas, treats a group of villagers on Ky Hoa Island off the coast near Chu Lai. The MEDCAP operation (Medical Civic Action Program) was an important part of the Marines' pacification efforts.

leg anymore?' How do you answer a youngster like that? And that probably was very difficult. Usually you'd sit down and try to help them write a letter, and try to say to them, 'Hey, you're still the man that they married. Maybe all of you is not there anymore, but she's still going to love you.' That was kind of difficult."

On May 10, elements of the 101st Airborne Division were airlifted into the A Shau Valley in an attempt to disrupt the communist infiltration routes which ran through the valley eastward to the coastal cities of northern Vietnam. Although they had been hearing rumors of a withdrawal, the men of the 101st continued to fight and die just as they had for the previous four years. And in the next few days, they would find themselves involved in one of the bloodiest battles of the war.

On May 12, the 3rd Battalion, 187th Regiment, 101st Airborne, swept along a ridge line on Hill 937, or Dong Ap Bia, as it was called by the Vietnamese. Soon, the U.S. troops would have a third name for it—Hamburger Hill—in reference to the many soldiers it would chew up in battle. As the battalion moved upward toward the peak, they came under heavy fire from entrenched communist forces and were forced to withdraw. This was the first of 11 assaults the U.S. troops would make

Left: *Medics carry a member of the 101st Airborne, wounded during the battle for Hamburger Hill, to a waiting medevac through a driving rainstorm. Below: A paratrooper from the 101st works furiously to save the life of a buddy seriously wounded during the fight for Hamburger Hill.*

Injured during an assault on Hamburger Hill, a soldier from the 101st grimaces as he awaits evacuation from a base camp.

against Hamburger Hill.

For the next eight days, 3rd Battalion, along with two other battalions from the 101st, tried again and again to take the hill, but the reportedly 1,500 members of two NVA regiments on the hill held firm. From their carefully constructed bunker system, they remained impervious to infantry charges, artillery and tactical air strikes.

Finally, on May 20, augmented by a fourth South Vietnamese battalion, the

Americans reached the top. In all, 46 Americans died capturing Hamburger Hill and another 300 were wounded. The U.S. command also listed 500 NVA killed. Although the fighting had stopped on the slopes of Hamburger Hill, the dispute over the battle itself was just beginning.

"A lot of people felt it was futile, of going up time and time again," said Patrick Power, 19, of Sunderland, Massachusetts, one of the men who fought

there. "There was a lot of anger over that. Everyone knew after the first company went up that we'd be walking into ambushes each and every time. A lot of people felt it was quite uncalled-for to be sent in every time they're ambushing. I didn't know anyone who wasn't frightened. It's just a matter of being nineteen or twenty years old and being scared not knowing, not having any control as to what's happening...."

"There were quite a few people who knew that they were going to die and they couldn't do anything about it. As a matter of fact, there was talk of not doing, of sitting back and essentially going on strike. But by the time it was five days into the battle, it was really total numbness. At the end of the battle, we had to identify the bodies or what there was left of them [and] bag them up for the next day.... I was just glad that I was out, and I think everyone was very elated that they were alive."

Paratroopers from the 101st await a medevac for a wounded soldier on the slope of Hamburger Hill. U.S. troops fought for ten days before taking the hill in a coordinated four-battalion assault.

Critics questioned whether Hamburger Hill was necessary. On the floor of the Senate, Massachusetts Senator Edward M. Kennedy charged that Hamburger Hill had no strategic value, calling the assault "senseless and irresponsible."

The U.S. military leaders staunchly defended their decision to attack Dong Ap Bia. "We found the enemy on Hill 937 [Ap Bia]," stated Major General Melvin Zais, who ordered the attack, "and that's where we fought him." General Westmoreland also defended the action arguing that "to have left the North Vietnamese undisturbed on the mountain would have been to jeopardize American control of the valley and accept a renewed threat to the coastal cities. A prolonged siege would have been costly and tied up troops indefinitely. The commander of the 101st, Major General Melvin Zais, quite properly ordered an attack."

Despite the military's defense of its actions on Dong Ap Bia, however, the outcome at home ultimately proved to be negative. Anti-war sentiment grew and support for the American withdrawal in the United States had received a large shot in the arm. On June 8, Nixon announced the first troop withdrawal.

Ironically, less than a month after the battle, NVA forces were reported moving back onto Hamburger Hill.

A vociferous opponent of the war during the late 60s, Senator Edward Kennedy denounces the rampant corruption in the GVN. Kennedy attacked the U.S. military's decision to take Hamburger Hill.

Above: *Major General Melvin Zais, commander of the 101st, who ordered the Dong Ap Bia be taken.* Below: *September 16, 1969. A Vietnamese boy in front of the Caravelle Hotel in Saigon hawks a newspaper announcing Nixon's decision to withdraw more than 40,000 more troops.*

Enjoying an infrequent visit to the city, soldiers from the U.S. camp at Bien Hoa take in the sights of Saigon from bicycle cabs. U.S. military leaders restricted access to Vietnam's cities in an attempt to minimize friction between soldiers and civilians.

U.S. soldiers relax on the "porch" of their armored personnel carrier (APC) in May, 1971. As the U.S. withdrawal continued, most U.S. troops still in the country were assigned to support duty.

A member of the 1st Air Cav washes his feet following a patrol 65 miles northwest of Saigon.

Above: Sporting Mohawk haircuts, Sergeant First Class Emmanual Bradford (left) of Seaside, California, and First Lieutenant Alfred E. Lehman Jr. of Schofield Barracks, Hawaii, settle down for some chow following a patrol near

Duc Pho. Below: Members of a 1st Infantry Division artillery unit stationed near Chanh Lau, 25 miles north of Saigon, enjoy a game of volleyball near their gun pit.

Margi Ness of Hinkley, Minnesota, plays a round of Back Alley with Marines at the Da Nang Red Cross Recreation Center. Although the U.S. military restricted the soldiers access to the cities, they attempted to provide for their needs with separate facilities such as this recreation center.

Specialist 4 James Smipes peddles through Saigon on a unicycle with his pet kitten on his shoulder.

Going Home

July 8, 1969. For the 814 men of the 3rd Battalion, 60th Infantry, this was a happy day, despite the heat of the sun beating down on them on the tarmac of Tan Son Nhut Air Base.

Young Vietnamese women, wearing brightly colored ao dais, gave each man a gaily wrapped gift box containing a small Vietnamese flag, a tape recording of Vietnamese songs and a gold shoulder cord for their uniforms. Around the soldiers' necks, they placed many-colored plastic leis.

In the festive atmosphere the G.I.s clowned around.

"I'm going home to momma where I belong," one man quipped.

Bemused by all the attention from newsmen, photographers and television cameramen, another joked, "My God, it's the first time the 9th Division has been overrun!"

The "Old Reliables" (the 9th Division's nickname) were leaving Vietnam, the first outfit to leave under President Nixon's new withdrawal plan. By the end of the year they would be joined by 29,000 other U.S. troops, with 50,000 more scheduled to return during the first four months of 1970.

Above: *U.S. Special Forces officers witness the transferral of the Special Forces camp at Duc Lap, one of the last two camps still operated by the United States in Vietnam, to the South Vietnamese in January, 1971.* Below: *G.I.s from the 11th Armored Cavalry Regiment fold up the flag at Camp Black Horse as the camp is turned over to the South Vietnamese.*

Above: *Four Vietnamese girls garbed in traditional ao dais drape leis around the necks of officers of the 101st Airborne in thanks for their service in Vietnam.* Below: *President Nixon mingles with soldiers from the 1st Infantry Division at their headquarters at Di An, 12 miles north of Saigon.*

President Nguyen Van Thieu (right) enjoys a drink with Ambassador Ellsworth Bunker. Bunker strongly supported U.S. policy in Vietnam following his succeeding Henry Cabot Lodge as ambassador in 1967.

Above: *Thieu and Prime Minister Nguyen Cao Ky express their agreement to a U.S. withdrawal at a news conference in April, 1968. Thieu made it clear at that time, however, that he did not want to see them go.* Below: *U.S. Special Forces troops shake hands with their South Vietnamese counterparts during ceremonies marking the transferral of the base to the GVN.*

"You have fought well," General Creighton Abrams told them, "under some of the most arduous and unusual combat conditions ever experienced by American soldiers. You are a credit to your generation."

As the men headed for the transports, they filed past their commander, Lieutenant Colonel Peter B. Petersen, of Chicago.

Occasionally, Petersen grasped the hand of a sergeant or enlisted man.

"You're looking good, men, you always did," he would say.

"You did a fine job."

"I'm damn proud of you."

"You're the best damn battalion in the Army."

Petersen fell out and ran ahead of the column to the waiting transports.

OME TOM

He picked up a covered coat hanger with his well-pressed civilian clothes from his headquarters staff.

"Okay, aircraft No. 1, let's go," he yelled.

After more than 20 years of growing involvement in Vietnam, the United States was finally starting on the way home.

Above: *Having escaped from the Viet Cong after 14 months of captivity, 21-year-old Michigan native Specialist 5 Thomas Van Putten returns home to a hero's welcome. Not all returning G.I.s received such a friendly reception.* Right: *Specialist 5 Don Shillow raises his bags in exhilaration as he steps off his plane from Saigon at Travis Air Force Base near Sacramento, California.*

CHAPTER 10
THE LAST TO DIE

For five days in August of 1969, A Company of the 196th Light Infantry Brigade's 3rd Battalion had tried to push down the jungle-covered, razor-edged slope of Nui Lon Mountain into a treacherous maze of North Vietnamese bunkers in the Song Chang Valley. Each time they were driven back. Now, Lieutenant Colonel Robert Bacon, who had taken over the battalion, was personally leading three of his companies in yet another assault down the slope. While he was waiting for A Company to move out, he received a call over a field telephone from A Company's commander.

"I am sorry, sir, but my men refused to go—we cannot move out," Lieutenant Eugene Shurtz, Jr. reported.

"Repeat that please," replied Bacon. "Have you told them what it means to disobey orders under fire?"

"I think they understood," Shurtz said. "But some of them simply had enough—they are broken. There are boys here who have only 90 days left in Vietnam. They want to go home in one piece. The situation is psychic here."

"Are you talking about enlisted men, or are the NCOs [noncommissioned officers] also involved?" the colonel asked.

"That's the difficulty here," Shurtz replied. "We've got a leadership problem. Most of our squad and platoon leaders have been killed or wounded."

"Go talk to them again and tell them that to the best of our knowledge the bunkers are now empty—the enemy has withdrawn," Bacon told the lieutenant. "The mission of A Company today is to recover their dead. They have no reason to be afraid. Please take a hand count of how many really do not want to go."

"They won't go, colonel, and I did not ask for the hand count because I am afraid that they all stick together even though some might prefer to go," Shurtz said.

"Leave these men on the hill and take your CP [command post] element and move to the objective," Bacon ordered the lieutenant.

"What do we do with the ammunition supplies?" Shurtz asked. "Shall we destroy them?"

Two South Vietnamese corpsmen wade through a stream in Kien Hoa Province, 40 miles south of Saigon. They are part of a South Vietnamese unit which had assumed responsiblity for an area previously assigned to the U.S. 9th Infantry, which had withdrawn six months earlier.

Above left: *Members of the 2nd Battalion, 17th Cavalry, 101st Airborne, fire at NVA snipers while on patrol south of the DMZ.*
Below: *A soldier from the 198th Light Infantry Brigade, part of the Americal Division, dashes for cover as his squad takes fire from an NVA outfit north of Quang Ngai.*

"Leave it with them," the colonel replied.

Bacon then ordered his executive officer, Major Richard Waite, and an experienced Vietnam soldier, Sergeant Okey Blakenship of Panther, West Virginia, to talk to A Company.

"Give them a pep talk and a kick in the butt," Bacon ordered the major and sergeant. Major Waite and Sergeant Blakenship found the half-strength unit of 60 men bearded and exhausted, their uniforms ripped and caked with dirt as they sat in the tall elephant grass.

"One of them was crying," said Blakenship.

The men of A Company, 19- and 20-year-old draftees, said they were being pushed too hard on too little sleep. They feared they might be wiped out. They had had enough of the blazing heat, the C rations in cans, the firefights and the rocket and mortar attacks. One of the men yelled at Blakenship that his company had suffered too much and that it should not have to go on. The sergeant lied to him, telling him that

another company was down to 15 men and was still on the move.

"Why did they do it?" the soldier asked.

"Maybe they have got something a little more than what you have got," the sergeant replied.

"Don't call us cowards, we are not cowards," the soldier shot back, running toward the sergeant with his fists clenched. Blakenship walked away to where the company commander was waiting. The soldiers in A Company picked up their rifles and followed him down the bomb-cratered slope. They were back in action again.

But A Company's initial refusal was a reflection of changing attitudes in 1969 and the early 1970s. More and more the men fighting in Vietnam began to question America's role there and to see the conflict as a standoff, a war of attrition with no end in sight. The war that Tom Davis had known in 1961 had changed, and so had the views of the men fighting it. No soldier wanted to be the last to die in Vietnam.

Above: *Strapping on extra rounds, a soldier from the 25th Infantry Division prepares to go out on patrol along the Cambodian border. Behind him, another soldier tests a Starlite infra-red night sight which has been attached to an M-14.*

While on leave at his home in Salamanca, New York, in the winter of 1969, 19-year-old Keith Franklin left a sealed envelope with his parents. He told them not to open it until after his death.

"You'll be back after your two years in service and we'll open the letter, read it then, and have a good laugh about it," Mrs. Charles Franklin told her son.

At the end of his furlough, Franklin shipped back to Vietnam. The following spring, he died there. His parents opened the envelope and found a letter addressed to them:

"Dear Mom and Dad:

"The war that has taken my life, and many thousands of others before me, is immoral, unlawful and an atrocity unlike any misfit of good sense and judgment known to man.... So, as I lie dead, please grant my last request. Help me to inform the American people —the silent majority who have not yet voiced their opinions. Help me let them know that their silence is permitting this atrocity to go on and that my death will not be in vain if by

prompting them to act I can in some way help to bring an end to the war that brought an end to my life?"

Lieutenant William Ahearn, 26, of Port Chester, New York, led an American mobile advisory team (MAT) in the Mekong Delta village of Tuan Tuc, south of Can Tho. His seven-member team lived in the village, training its residents to function as soldiers during the night when the VC attacked. In a letter home dated March 5, 1970, he described the quandary of the U.S. soldiers then fighting in Vietnam.

The names of the ships (U.S. helicopters) vary: Tiger Surprise, Viking, T-Bird, Lucky Strike, Super Slick. Their jobs are the same: to hunt down VC, to break up any VC attack. I have never met any of them, yet their voices are very familiar. We have used them in our area many times. We have heard their voices over the radio each evening—laughed many, many times at their conversations with each other . . . their kidding, boasting about their ships, women, how much time left in country. They are a lively bunch of men.

A call for help went out to two of those

133

ships—Lucky Strike and Super Slick. Romeo, the MAT five miles south of us, had two outposts under full attack. The VC were hitting the outposts with all they had, gunships were needed to save them. Since it is all open flat land here, we could see the tracer bullets being exchanged between the VC and the outposts. With a pair of binoculars, we could even make out rockets being fired. We heard the call go out for gunships and one passed overhead. He was soon over the battle area and his high-beam spotlight went on in search of the enemy. It went out as he began to receive enemy fire. The ship was Super Slick. Another ship passed overhead, and I hurried inside to the radio to listen.

"Romeo, Romeo—Lucky Strike, Lucky Strike!"

"Lucky Strike, this is Romeo, over."

"This is Strike, roger . . . what have you got for me? Over."

"This is Romeo. Two outposts under VC attack from the west. Over."

"Strike, roger. Out."

"Strike, this is Super Slick. Over."

"Hey . . . Slick. What's happening?"

"This is Slick. I'm at 900 and on blackout. Received some automatic weapons fire from below. Over."

134

There was no immediate answer. I called again.

"Gulf. This is Super Slick. Lucky Strike was hit, blew up in the air."

His voice was shaking. Someone else called him and asked him if there were any survivors. Again no immediate answer. Then Slick broke in:

"Negative. Impossible for anyone to survive that."

My men kept yelling at me that it had to be one of the ships. I told them it was Strike. They could not believe it. I could not believe it. He was alive as he flew over our place. Now he was dead—and so was his crew of five men. We stood there and looked out to where Strike had gone down. A lone red beacon flashed overhead . . . Super Slick. I knew how he felt. There was nothing that could be done. A few minutes later the air was full of helicopters and another cry came on the radio:

"T-Bird 1 is down. He's down. Let's get in there."

This time three men were picked up from another ship shot down, a fourth was crushed under the ship, which later blew up. Seven Americans killed in less than 20 minutes. It was too much for my men to take and for the choppers in the area:

"Romeo. This is T-Bird 3. Be advised we are going to blow this place to hell."

And they did. Ship after ship—five to ten of them—passed over the area and tossed in rockets and steady machine gun fire.

"Sir, let's go in there!" yelled one of my men. "Let's get some men and go in there."

I, too, wanted to go. We wanted to do something. We all had that instant courage—or insanity—that comes when you see a fellow American killed. We could not go. It was too far and we would be ambushed. The courage soon turned to anger. We were all cursing out the VC. Then the anger turned to our Vietnamese counterparts.

"Seven dead," said another of the men. "For what? These people don't appreciate a damn thing. They take, take, take . . . don't give a thing."

This went on and on. Uncontrolled anger, emotion. I felt it. My men felt it. I wanted to kill. They wanted to kill. Finally, the anger gave way to silence. My men went to bed. I stayed outside and watched the many red beacons in that area. There were no more cries on the radio. No more rockets or bullets. I still could not grasp that Lucky Strike was dead. The next morning few words passed among any of us.

President Thieu was to appear in the hamlet north of us, the one we had given the desks to. He would be there at 10:00 a.m. to hand out land titles, school kits, farming tools. I had to go. I asked my men if they wanted to go. They said no. I knew why. I had to go.

I am told friends cannot be afforded in a war. Perhaps it is true. I am tired of going from knowing to remembering.

Left: *A Huey Cobra gunship pulls out of a strafing run on a VC position near Cao Lanh in the Mekong Delta. The explosions are white phosphorous rockets fired from the helicopter's rocket launcher.* Below: *Dangling some 1,500 feet above the Song Thu Bon River, south of Da Nang, members of a Marine recon group hang from an evacuation ladder after being extracted from an ambush by communist forces.*

"This is Strike. Roger. I'll be coming in at 700. Beacon on. I'll try and find them. Over."

I went back outside to watch Strike put on his beam. Before any lights came on, a huge red fireball appeared in the air and went groundward. It had to be one of the ships—I ran in and called Super Slick.

"Super Slick—This is Gulf. Did one of you just go down? Over."

MY LAI

Task force commander Lieutenant Colonel Frank A. Barker called the action on March 16, 1968, a search-and-destroy mission that was "well planned, well executed and successful." The rest of the world called it the My Lai massacre.

During a few hot and humid morning hours in the Vietnamese hamlet of My Lai 4, part of Song My village in the province of Quang Tri, the men of Charlie Company, 1st Battalion, 11th Brigade, 20th Infantry Regiment, Americal Division, slew scores of unarmed, unresisting Vietnamese civilians. Estimates of the number killed ran from 200, according to official Army sources, to more than 500, according to local villagers.

For more than a year the story of what happened that morning in My Lai 4 remained untold.

Finally, in March of 1969, Ron Ridenhour, a Vietnam veteran who had learned of the massacre from several of the men of Charlie Company, mailed letters to 30 military and congressional leaders documenting his belief that "something rather dark and bloody did indeed occur sometime in March, 1968, in a village called 'Pinkville' [My Lai] in the Republic of Vietnam." Seven months later, on November 12, 1969, Lieutenant William L. Calley, Jr., commander of Charlie Company, faced an Army court-martial, charged with the murder of 109 Vietnamese civilians (later dropped to 102). The "dark and bloody" secret was finally out in the open.

Although massacres and atrocities—on both sides—were not unknown in Vietnam, as in any war, the My Lai disclosures shocked a nation that prided itself on honor. Senator Daniel K. Inouye, a Democrat from Hawaii who had lost an arm in World War II, was horrified after seeing pictures of the massacre. "Having been in combat myself, I thought I would be hardened, but I must say I am a bit sickened."

For four months in the small, neat courtroom at Fort Benning, Georgia, the whys and wherefores of My Lai were examined in minute detail through the testimony of 91 witnesses and by means of hundreds of depositions, documents, maps and photographs.

One prosecution witness, Paul Meadlo, a 23-year-old rifleman in Calley's platoon, testified that as the first platoon entered My Lai, he helped round up about 35 or 40 Vietnamese men, women and children who were then herded at rifle point into a clearing where two trails crossed the village.

Meadlo quoted Calley's order to him: "You know what to do with them, Meadlo."

"I assumed he meant guard them, and I said, 'Yes,'" Meadlo testified.

When Calley returned, he asked, "How come they're not dead?"

"I said I didn't know we were supposed to kill them," Meadlo testified, then quoted Calley's response as, "I want them dead."

"He told me to help shoot them," Meadlo added.

Meadlo said he and Calley stood side by side and fired into the captives with M-16s from a distance of about 20 feet. The Army had estimated that at least 30 Vietnamese were massacred there and another 70 villagers in an L-shaped ditch on

Lieutenant William L. Calley. Pictured here during his court-martial at Fort Benning, Georgia. Calley was the only U.S. officer convicted for his actions during the My Lai incident.

The bodies of women and children lay piled on a road leading from My Lai.

the eastern edge of the village. Meadlo placed that number at 75 to 100.

"He [Calley] said to me, 'We got another job to do, Meadlo.' Lieutenant Calley started shoving them off and shooting them in the ravine."

Another witness, Dennis Conti, 21, testified he had helped Meadlo guard the Vietnamese on the trail and saw Calley fire upon them as "they screamed and yelled." He said Meadlo began to weep and tried to get him to join in the massacre.

"I said, 'If they're gonna be killed, let Lieutenant Calley do it. I'm not gonna do it.' Lieutenant Calley fired on 'em and killed 'em one by one."

Conti said he watched Calley firing at the massed Vietnamese cowering in the ditch. "A lot of them were trying to get up," he testified. "Most were just screaming. They were shot up pretty bad. I looked down and seen a woman trying to get up. I seen Lieutenant Calley fire and blow the side of her head off."

In his defense, Calley said, "If I've committed a crime, the only crime I have committed is in judgment of my values—apparently I have valued my troops' lives more than I did that of the enemy. When my troops were getting massacred and mauled by an enemy I couldn't see, I couldn't feel and I couldn't touch, that nobody in the military ever described as anything other than communism.

"They didn't give it a race, they didn't give it a sex, they didn't give it an age. They never let me believe it was just a philosophy in a man's mind. That was my enemy out there and when it came between me and that enemy, I had to value the lives of my troops, and I feel that is the only crime I have committed."

Despite his plea, Calley was convicted at the end of March, 1971 by a jury of six senior officers of first-degree murder of at least 22 villagers. He was sentenced to life imprisonment. That sentence was reduced five months later by President Nixon to 20 years. Calley actually served three years under house arrest at Fort Benning.

The unpopularity of the war spawned a breakdown in discipline and a polarization of American military ranks. On one side were the officers and noncommissioned officers, the career men call "lifers." On the other side were the draftees, who felt that they were being used and hassled.

Drug abuse became a major problem. In 1965, the Army apprehended 47 servicemen for using drugs. By 1970, that figure reached 11,000, and even at that, the command believed that for every soldier caught, five went undetected. Eleven drug rehabilitation centers were set up in Vietnam, and by late 1971 urinalysis was mandatory for all GIs leaving Vietnam. Those who did not pass the test were held up and placed in quarantine centers for detoxification before being sent home.

A U.S. Army officer looks over a display of drugs confiscated at Can Tho airfield in the Mekong Delta area in 1971. Plentiful and cheap, drugs provided a convenient, easy way to forget the war.

The most disturbing development of the burgeoning disciplinary problems within the military in Vietnam was the practice of "fragging." Taken from the word "fragmentation," fragging involved the use of violence—usually a grenade (which could not be traced) thrown into a "hootch" (living quarters), or a bullet in the back during a firefight—to settle disputes between soldiers and their officers or NCOs. If a soldier felt he was being hassled or asked to perform unnecessarily hazardous duty, he could simply kill whoever was giving the orders. Sometimes there was a warning—a tear gas canister dropped inside a hootch—sometimes not.

From 1969 to 1971, the Army reported more than 600 fragging incidents resulting in 82 deaths and 651 injuries. In 1971 alone there were 1.8 fragging incidents for every 1,000 U.S.

138

U.S. soldiers line up at Long Binh base to give urine samples at a heroin detection

soldiers serving in Vietnam (not including gun and knife assaults).

The most frightening aspect of the practice of fragging in Vietnam, however, was its apparent randomness.

Other wars had seen soldiers kill their commanding officer if they felt he was taking too many chances with their lives. But in Vietnam, as one officer put it, "All it takes is a 'How are you,

center. All G.I.s were required to take the test, prior to leaving for home. Those who didn't pass had to undergo detoxification.

Joe,' and bang, someone will shoot you."

One unit reported two men killed and 17 more wounded in fragging incidents. The unit's commander, a brigadier general, took to sleeping with a machine gun under his bed. His explanation: "I don't trust my guards."

As the United States continued to disengage itself from this, its longest war, the war effort continued to lose support both at home and in Vietnam. Disillusionment and resentment ran deep among many of the men serving there. For many of them the end could not come soon enough.

CHAPTER 11
CAMBODIA AND LAOS

The young American soldier, named Cliff, looked up numbly from the field operating table. Beside him stood Jackie Navarra, an Army nurse.

"Hi," said Jackie.

"Wow," said Cliff, "and I didn't even take a shower."

"Cliff . . . "

"How did you know my name? I used to be pretty good-looking."

Within a few minutes, Cliff, who had just lost both his legs and his right arm, would be dead despite the efforts of four surgeons to save his life.

"He was thankful to be alive," said Jackie, "and didn't realize what happened. His legs were folded up on his chest. He could see his right arm folded back. He was pretty cool under anesthetics. Everybody tried to keep the anxiety out of their voices."

At age 22, Jackie Navarra came right from nursing school in Albion, New York, to Vietnam to treat dozens of soldiers like Cliff in a field hospital in the monsoons and mud of Quang Tri City, just below the demilitarized zone. To her, Quang Tri was a bummer, but she had come anyhow to support the soldiers who didn't like being in Vietnam any more than she did. It was stressful but it was worth it. She would never feel more worthwhile in her life, she thought.

"It's really depressing because of the amputations," she was saying. "What a waste of men. After the cases are through, everything comes back to you. I'm not old-fashioned. If I knew what we were fighting for, if the enemy did something to our country, I could see it. I don't know why we're here. So many G.I.s ask why. I can't answer. I came because I knew they needed medical help here. I wanted to appreciate things better back home, like clean sheets, running water and also a happy family."

At the start of 1970, the war ground on, as deadly as ever. Although the number of U.S. troops in Vietnam declined steadily, and the South Vietnamese assumed more and more of the burden of the fighting, the war continued to take its toll on U.S. servicemen —335 dead in January, 385 in February, 442 in March.

In Paris, the stalemated peace talks continued to offer no hope for an early settlement, and on the battlefield, neither side seemed able to gain an edge. Then at the end of April, in the most dramatic turn in the war since Tet, a new chapter was opened in the war's history.

On April 30, President Nixon appeared on national television to tell America that a combined U.S. and South Vietnamese force had invaded Cambodia. Ten days earlier he had announced his plan to withdraw 150,000 troops over the next 12 months.

"I have concluded the time has come for action," Nixon declared. He said moves by the North Vietnamese and Viet Cong "in the last ten days closely endanger the lives of Americans who are in Vietnam now and would constitute an unacceptable risk to those who would be there after our withdrawal of 150,000.

"We take this action," he continued, "not for the purpose of expanding the war into Cambodia but for the purpose of ending the war in Vietnam and winning the just peace we . . . desire."

The invasion, christened Total Victory, was aimed at the communist sanctuaries along the eastern edge of Cambodia. For the previous year, in a secret bombing campaign code-named Menu, U.S. B-52s had

Facing page: *A U.S. armored column heads along Route 9 near the Laotian border while a Chinook helicopter transporting a 105mm howitzer stirs up a cloud of dust just over the rise. The U.S. troops are moving to support the South Vietnamese invasion of Laos, Lam Son 719, in March, 1971. Top: A young G.I. from the U.S. 25th Infantry Division weeps from exhaustion in the midst of a firefight outside the village of Tasuos in Cambodia.*

Left: *Prince Norodom Sihanouk of Cambodia. For 20 years, the Cambodian ruler safely navigated his country through the storms and tempests of Southeast Asian politics.* Middle: *"Vain and flighty" said Richard Nixon of Sihanouk, yet the young prince outwitted first the French, who thought to make him a puppet ruler, and then opposition from within Cambodia before finally being ousted in March, 1970.* Right: *Premier Lon Nol. An idealist who felt that Cambodia should ally itself with the United States, Lon Nol chafed at Sihanouk's failure to rid Cambodia of the Vietnamese communists operating from bases inside Cambodia along the South Vietnamese border.*

pounded the sanctuaries with no apparent results. At the time, Cambodia's leader, Prince Norodom Sihanouk, had voiced no public protest over the bombing but had refused to allow either U.S. or Vietnamese troops to cross the border.

For years, Sihanouk had negotiated an uncertain neutrality, refusing to align himself with either the United States or the communists. In March 1970, however, that neutrality would come to an end. While Sihanouk vacationed in France, a pro-U.S. faction led by General Lon Nol deposed the absent leader. The new government, headed by Lon Nol, ordered the North Vietnamese and Viet Cong out of the country and turned to the United States for assistance. The door had been opened for the invasion.

On April 29, ARVN units assaulted the Parrot's Beak area of Cambodia, 30 miles west of Saigon. Two days later, a combined U.S.-South Vietnamese force launched a similar invasion into Cambodia's Fishhook area, 70 miles northwest of Saigon. The two forces totaled more than 20,000 troops. At the invasion's height, that figure would

A South Vietnamese armored column passes through a Cambodian Army checkpoint at the heavily damaged town of Tonle Bet, 45 miles northeast of Phnom Penh.

142

reach 63,000 (23,000 of whom would be Americans).

Initially, U.S. and South Vietnamese forces met only token resistance. As U.S. planes and helicopters filled the sky overhead, U.S. tanks and armored personnel carriers (APCs) rumbled through the Cambodian countryside unchallenged. Although the United States had sought to keep the invasion a secret, the communists had somehow received advance warning, allowing them to flee westward prior to the invasion.

Snuol

Although most allied units made only light contacts with the North Vietnamese, on May 5, elements of the 11th Armed Cavalry Regiment encountered stiff opposition at the town of Snuol, north of the Fishhook area. Considered a center of communist activity, Snuol had been singled out as a prime objective during the first part of the invasion.

Prior to the battle, the commander of the armored column, Lieutenant Colonel Grail Brookshire, 37, of Stone Mountain, Georgia, had told his men, "If you take fire, return it. If you take fire and you look like you've got prepared positions, back 'em out—shoot and back out. Then we're just going to have to start prepping it [with air strikes]. . . ." His instructions were carried out to the letter.

As the 25 Sheridan tanks and APCs blasted their way into the center of Snuol, deeply entrenched North Viet-

South Vietnamese troops prepare to board a squadron of Hueys which will take them into Cambodia for an assault against the North Vietnamese 88th Regiment.

Above: *June 2, 1970. A South Vietnamese armored vehicle approaches a burning APC outside the town of Snuol.* Below: *Two Vietnamese soldiers armed with M-16s stand guard while their patrol searches through an abandoned village near Krek in the Fishhook area of Cambodia.*

Above: *Aerial view of the destroyed town of Snuol. Below: As a hut burns in the background, GVN soldiers sweep through a Cambodian hamlet near Snuol in February, 1971. Although South Vietnamese troops continued to operate in Cambodia following the U.S. withdrawal, communist troops still maintained base camps in the border areas.*

South Vietnamese troops await transport at Ah Hoa. These troops are scheduled to take part in a sweep near the Laotian border just below the DMZ, an area previously patrolled by U.S. troops.

Above: *Men of the U.S. Army's 23rd Artillery Group fire a 175mm against suspected VC targets in South Vietnam. Below: U.S. Army Chinook lifts a slingload of ammunition and supplies from Firebase Speer in Cambodia as U.S. forces rush to meet the June 30 deadline on operations in Cambodia imposed by President Nixon.*

namese soldiers unleashed a fearsome barrage, forcing the Americans to retreat. U.S. jet bombers and helicopter gunships now took over, battering the picturesque town.

When the U.S. troops moved back in, they found the town destroyed. Almost 90 percent had been laid to waste. Two blocks of ten-story concrete buildings now formed two huge piles of rubble. In the town square, they found the charred bodies of a girl, a woman and two men. Lieutenant Colonel Brookshire said he was ordered to attack the town because it was a North Vietnamese supply hub. "We had no choice but to take it," he said.

Within two weeks of the attack on Snuol, the U.S. command began withdrawing troops from Cambodia. By the end of June all of the American units had pulled out, although some 10,000 South Vietnamese and their American advisers remained.

Some of the American troops flew back to Vietnam. Others walked or rode. All were happy to be leaving and returning to their camps, where hot meals, beer and letters from home awaited them. "It feels good to see somebody from back in the world," said Sergeant Terry Coleman, 24, of Santa Rosa, California.

During the Cambodian invasion, the allied command claimed more than 11,000 NVA and VC killed and another 2,000 captured while listing its own losses at 339 Americans and 799 South Vietnamese killed. More impressive and more important in the eyes of the U.S. military leaders was the damage done to the communist supply system. Among other things, allied troops captured more than 25,000 weapons, 15 million rounds of ammunition and more than 7,000 tons of food—the

A soldier from the U.S. 4th Infantry displays a case of brand-new American-made .45 caliber pistols captured at a communist base camp in Cambodia's Se San River Valley, 50 miles west of Pleiku.

Carrying flags and signs proclaiming their support for President Nixon, hard-hat workers jam the City Hall area in New York City. Their rally came in response to the many other demonstrations and rallies around the country opposing the U.S. invasion of Cambodia.

equivalent of 4,000 truckloads of war materials sent down the Ho Chi Minh trail. Senior American officials estimated that these losses would set back North Vietnamese and Viet Cong operations six months, buying the South Vietnamese precious time to develop and improve its army. For this reason, they hailed the invasion as a success.

Again, however, as in the Tet offensive, there were political as well as military repercussions from what happened on the battlefield. Domestic reaction to the invasion in the United States had been swift. Demonstrations and student strikes erupted at nearly one-third of the nation's 2,500 college and university campuses. At Kent State University in Ohio, National Guardsmen killed four students

and wounded nine others during a student protest. At Jackson, Mississippi, police killed two during student demonstrations on the Jackson State College campus.

During the planning of the invasion, General Douglas Kinnard had opposed the operation.

"My feeling at the time was, and I said this to our State Department adviser the night before, sitting in my little office there, that politically this was a mistake. It was going to cause enormous problems at home. I didn't foresee, of course, Kent State. [This was] a psychological war, a political war, and again, the home front erupted."

Despite rekindling opposition to the war in the United States, the Cambodian invasion did allow the United

States time to implement its Vietnamization policy. Following the invasion, the United States withdrew all of its troops from the border region for good, replacing two and a half American divisions stationed there with South Vietnamese troops. By September, American combat divisions such as the 25th and the 1st Air Cavalry conducted only mopping-up operations. South Vietnamese battle deaths soared to four times those of the Americans, and only in the northernmost provinces bordering on Laos and the DMZ did the United States actively participate in combat operations. By January, 1971 336,000 U.S. troops remained in Vietnam with more scheduled for withdrawal. Slowly, the United States was working itself out of a job.

Above: *Demonstrators flee across the commons at Kent State University as National Guardsmen move toward them.* Below left: *Bending over a fallen student hit by fire from the Guardsmen, students confront the gas-masked soldiers.* Below right: *Students try to staunch the flow of blood from William K. Schroeder, one of four students killed by the National Guardsmen at Kent State.*

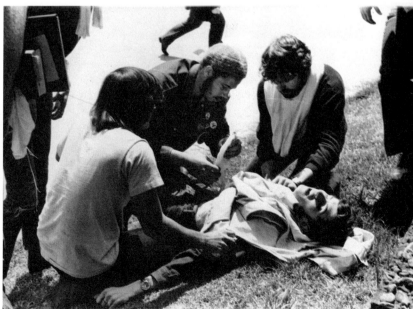

Lam Son 719

The first major test of the combat effectiveness of the South Vietnamese forces came in February and March of 1971 during an operation into Laos called Lam Son 719. Its objective was to cut the Ho Chi Minh trail, the main infiltration route from North Vietnam into the south. This time, however, there were no American ground troops sent into Laos. Instead, the dwindling American ground forces like the 5th Mechanized Infantry supported the South Vietnamese from bases on the Vietnamese side of the border. Only U.S. planes and helicopters would provide any support for the South Vietnamese inside Laos.

Sergeant Louis Forrisi, a member of the 3rd Squadron, 5th Cavalry, 1st Brigade, of the 5th Mechanized, took part in one of the U.S. support operations for Lam Son 719. His unit was assigned reconnaissance duty for the brigade's engineer battalion. His outfit operated in the "Punch Bowl," a large, grassy valley surrounded by jungle-covered mountains near Khe Sanh.

"Our first day in the Punch Bowl was to search for another one of these phantom NVA artillery spotters that higher-ups say are calling rounds into Khe Sanh," Forrisi wrote in his diary. "So someone gets the idea he's in a group of trees in the middle of the place . . . Khe Sanh is miles away up in the hills and here we are far below it on a valley floor. But we are ordered to assault this treeline. The lieutenant plays the game by lining up the platoon and letting go with everything we have for about five minutes. After this show, we dismount and walk through what is now a burned out bunch of trees and all that's there is two dead snakes.

"Every night we move to one of the three positions the engineers prepared for us while they were cutting the road at the beginning of the operation. The ground surveillance team is with us constantly now. And then radar picks up movement every night, but at long ranges. So we lob a few mortar shells in that area and find nothing there in the morning.

"Every day we'd patrol a different area of the Punch Bowl, checking out the woods or under the culverts the engineers put under the road to prevent washouts. The night went by quietly. It was like the war didn't exist."

For the Americans flying support for the ARVN troops in Laos, however, it was still business as usual. During the operation, 66 helicopter pilots and crewmen were killed, 83 more were wounded, and another 28 were listed as missing. Bobby Gunn, a 20-year-old helicopter pilot from Manor, Georgia,

had tried for four days to recover the bodies of several Americans killed in the hills of Laos, supporting the South Vietnamese. On the fifth day, Gunn had a brush with death.

"I saw tracers coming up just right in front of the helicopter," he said. "I pressed the intercom on the floor. I told the rest of the people in the helicopter we were taking fire. At the time I got the words out of my mouth, a round came through the chin bubble, the lower part of the Plexiglas windshield. I assumed it deflected off the metal strip along the bubble. It came in my

Above: *South Vietnamese interpreter directs U.S. Cobra gunships on attack runs against communist positions in Laos. U.S. helicopters suffered heavy casualties in the operation.* Facing page: *Troops from the Americal Division head toward the abandoned U.S. Special Forces camp at Lang Vei aboard APCs. They are assuming support positions for the South Vietnamese invasion of Laos, Lam Son 719.*

helmet, went up three or four inches, and stopped. The metal strip slowed it down. I didn't know exactly what happened. The Plexiglas blew up in my face. The sergeant, when he saw I was hit, helped take off the helmet, and a .51-caliber round fell out. That's my souvenir. I'm going to keep my helmet, too. I'll get a new one. That was damn close. It scared the hell out of me."

The 46-day operation ended in disaster for the South Vietnamese. Badly beaten from the start, ARVN troops quickly found themselves on the defensive. Soldiers clung desperately to

the skids of helicopters in efforts to escape the North Vietnamese slaughter. Losses ran as high as 50 percent. At the end of the operation on March 25, the South Vietnamese counted 3,000 men dead or missing and 7,000 wounded. One of the regiments from the crack 1st Division returned with only 450 of its 2,000 men still in fighting condition. In one battalion of 500 men, only 32 survived and a third of them were wounded.

Three years before, South Vietnamese divisions languished in the cities while American forces fought the major

battles and died. Now, in their first major head-on battle with the NVA, they had been battered.

The Laotian operation underscored two major weaknesses of the Vietnamization program—heavy reliance on American air support and lack of an adequate supply system. U.S. and South Vietnamese officials acknowledged the drive into Laos could never have been launched and sustained without massive U.S. air support. Many now openly wondered how long the South Vietnamese could hope to survive once the United States left.

149

CHAPTER 12
PEACE, NO PEACE

The townspeople of An Loc were at church services on a clear day in April, 1972 when they heard the distant rumble. As the services continued, the noise grew louder, eventually becoming a roar. Suddenly, North Vietnamese tanks crashed through the church's walls. As the worshipers turned to flee, the tanks turned the church into a scene of carnage, firing upon the people with their cannons and machine guns.

"They annihilated well over 100 civilians, mostly women and children," said Captain Harold Moffett Jr., a 29-year-old Army adviser from Nashville, Tennessee, who survived the two-month siege of the provincial capital 60 miles north of Saigon that followed.

"There was nothing to do except look at it and continue to fight," Moffett said. "That's a terrible thing to say, but it's true. In a situation like that you can't be horrified. You've got to maintain your sense and bearing. If you lose your senses, you've lost yourself."

South Vietnamese soldiers weighing as little as 80 pounds stood up against the 80,000-pound tanks with nothing more than a 3-pound antitank weapon.

In one night, the North Vietnamese poured 10,000 rounds of artillery, rockets and mortars into the city, leaving it in ruins, pockmarked with craters. For 10 hours, the shells fell without letup, nearly 20 rounds a minute. Moffett didn't think ahead. He lived hour to hour, round to round.

"I never dreamed anything like that was possible, to put so many rounds in one small area in such a short period of time. We used to count the rounds as they came in by the hour, starting a new count each hour. But they increased and increased so much we couldn't keep up."

He thought, "I hope we don't get a direct hit." He had a close call when a rocket tore through an air vent in his bunker. Miraculously, he survived more than 50,000 rounds with only a slight wound in his back from a mortar fragment.

1972 had begun with high hopes for peace. In Vietnam, the northeast winter monsoons helped reduce fighting to a low point at the beginning of the

---

The terror of war. A group of terrified South Vietnamese children flee down Route 1 following an accidental napalm attack by GVN planes. The girl at center had ripped off her burning clothes as she fled. (Pulitzer Prize photo by Nguyen Kong (Nick) Ut, 1972.)

South Vietnamese troops along Route 13 look toward An Loc where an NVA outfit has ambushed a GVN ammunition convoy during the Easter offensive. Below: A South Vietnamese medic tends to GVN troops wounded in a North Vietnamese ambush along Route 13. The South Vietnamese suffered heavy casualties before turning back the communists with the help of heavy U.S. tactical air support.

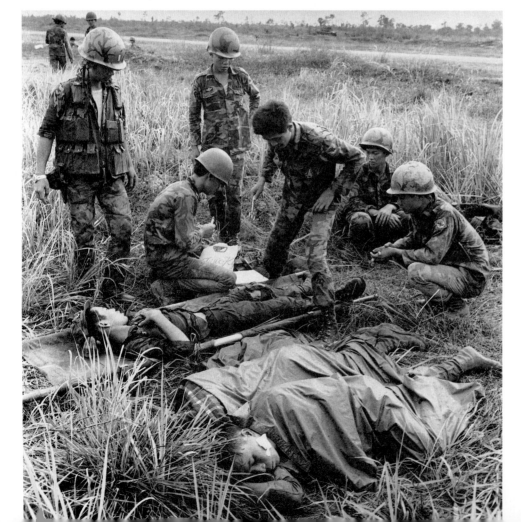

year. In Paris, although peace talks had broken off in November, President Nixon's national security adviser, Henry Kissinger, had managed to keep the lines of communication open, meeting a dozen times in secret with North Vietnamese officials. President Nixon even announced a new, more conciliatory eight-point peace plan.

The Easter Offensive

In what analysts believed was an attempt to discredit Nixon's Vietnamization plan and to gain an advantage at the peace talks, the North Vietnamese launched a major spring offensive on Easter weekend against South Vietnamese bases and provincial and district capitals including Quang Tri, just below the DMZ, and An Loc. They steamrolled over border outposts north of Kontum in the Central Highlands and destroyed three-fourths of Binh Dinh province to the east along the coastal plain, threatening again to cut the country in half.

An Loc held. But at Quang Tri, waves of North Vietnamese infantrymen from the 304th Division swept across the DMZ with tanks and rolled over the inexperienced South Viet-

South Vietnamese troops from the Mekong Delta head toward the besieged city of An Loc. Below left: Laden for work, North Vietnamese delegates enter the house in the Paris suburb of Saint-Nom-La-Bretache, where they resumed secret peace negotiations with U.S. representatives in January, 1973.

namese 3rd Division. Newly formed to replace the withdrawing American forces, much of 3rd Division was destroyed in this, its first major engagement. Half of Quang Tri province, including the provincial capital of Quang Tri City, fell. It was seen as a major psychological victory for Hanoi, although the city was eventually retaken, much of it in ruins.

As they had prior to the 1968 Tet offensive, allied intelligence had received some warnings of a North Vietnamese buildup, but the evidence was not conclusive. Military commanders

President Nixon announces a more conciliatory peace plan on national television, January 25, 1972. The North Vietnamese response was to launch the Easter offensive.

153

Carrying a wounded soldier, South Vietnamese litter bearers walk through the ruins of Quang Tri City following the Easter offensive.

A Vietnamese man searches through the rubble looking for signs of his missing family. Thousands of soldiers and civilians were killed when North Vietnamese forces ambushed a convoy fleeing the city as other NVA units attacked.

A burned-out street in the provincial capital of Quang Tri reflects the bitter house-to-house fighting between GVN and NVA forces during the battle for the city. Below, South Vietnamese refugees flee the fighting at Quang Tri. As the war progressed, Vietnam came to be a nation of refugees.

Operation Linebacker I. U.S. jets attack targets at Haiphong Harbor during an airstrike launched in retaliation for the Easter offensive. President Nixon also ordered that North Vietnam's primary seaport be mined.

did not consider the threat dangerous enough to reinforce border units. Even when the North Vietnamese intensified their artillery attacks across the DMZ against the 3rd Division's forward posts, few thought there was any real cause for alarm. Military officials later said the surprise offensive would not have caught the 3rd Division off guard had it patrolled more aggressively.

The Easter offensive again brought home South Vietnam's heavy reliance on American firepower, which saved An Loc. The North Vietnamese offensive would have been a bigger rout had it not been for U.S. B-52 bombers and other American air support. Shifting their focus of attacks from Cambodia and Laos, the heavy bombers launched 6,000 missions between April and June in support of the beleaguered South Vietnamese at An Loc, Kontum and Quang Tri. At An Loc, B-52s struck less than 1,000 yards from the South Vietnamese defenses at some points as the North Vietnamese closed in.

Proof of the improved accuracy of U.S. bombs: a destroyed bridge two miles southwest of Dong Hoi, North Vietnam. The Linebacker airstrikes in response to the Easter invasion hit targets all across North Vietnam.

156

Smoke and shell fragments rise from burning ammunition dump at Kontum airfield on May 17. The ammunition had just been delivered by U.S. planes when a North Vietnamese rocket attack set it afire.

Smoke billows skyward from a South Vietnamese fuel dump hit by NVA rockets in the city of Kontum. Below: Cradling his puppy, a G.I. arrives with his unit in the besieged city of Kontum.

June 7. After 12 days of street fighting, GVN troops retake the city of Kontum. Much of the Central Highland capital was destroyed by allied air and artillery strikes.

General John Vogt, the commander of the U.S. 7th Air Force, said the B-52 strikes were essential to the defense efforts and made the difference at An Loc and Kontum. However, although the Kontum front had stabilized, a South Vietnamese division in the region was virtually destroyed, and by year's end, the North Vietnamese still controlled wide areas captured during the offensive.

President Nixon warned Hanoi to call off its offensive or face a resumption of the bombing in North Vietnam. The warning was ignored. In April, for the first time in four years, American bombers filled the skies of North Vietnam, and for the first time ever, B-52s joined in the bombing raids. At the same time, President Nixon ordered the mining of Haiphong and other North Vietnamese harbors in an effort to cut off Hanoi's supply lines from the Soviet Union and other communist bloc nations.

The peace talks resumed in July, and by fall, an agreement seemed near, with less than 50,000 American troops

Her infant twins safely ensconced in a bamboo basket, a Vietnamese mother enters a refugee camp south of Quang Tri.

157

South Vietnamese President Nguyen Van Thieu.

still in Vietnam. In August, the last U.S. combat unit in Vietnam, 3rd Battalion, 21st Infantry, 196th Light Infantry Brigade, departed for home. Finally, in early October, Kissinger reported that two stumbling blocks for the peace negotiations had been removed: Hanoi had dropped its demands for a coalition government in Saigon and for the ouster of President Thieu.

On October 26, with the 1972 presidential elections in the United States only a week and a half away, Kissinger declared, "Peace is at hand." A final agreement, he said, could be reached in one more negotiating session lasting not more than three or four days. In anticipation of the agreement, the United States restricted its air strikes to areas south of the 20th parallel, well below the Hanoi-Haiphong heartland.

However, South Vietnamese President Nguyen Van Thieu balked at the agreement. The proposal contained no provisions for the withdrawal of 145,000 North Vietnamese troops from the south, nor did it specify the exact role of the proposed National Council of Reconciliation and Concord that would include representatives of the

Saigon government, the Viet Cong and neutralists. Such an agreement, Thieu argued, would mean "a surrender of the South Vietnamese people to the communists." He pledged to fight alone if necessary.

Linebacker II

On December 18, fresh from a landslide election victory, President Nixon ordered massive air strikes against the heartland of North Vietnam in efforts to pressure Hanoi into reaching an agreement.

B-52 bombers, each carrying 40 tons

Above: *October 31. The table awaits the delegates expected to sign a peace agreement. Two days later, however, negotiations fell through and Nixon ordered Linebacker II, the heaviest aerial assault of the war, against North Vietnam. Left: This photo, released by East Germany, shows the ruins of a section of a hospital in Hanoi, hit during a B-52 bombing attack. U.S. B-52s flew more than 740 sorties against targets in North Vietnam during the 11 days of Linebacker II.*

Above: *October 26. Henry Kissinger informs the press at a White House news conference that peace is at hand. His pronouncement, however, came three months before the fact. Below: Nixon and Agnew accept the nomination of their party in Miami Beach on August 0.*

of bombs, flew through heavy North Vietnamese missile defenses to strike targets in the Hanoi-Haiphong region for the first time in the war. The biggest aerial blitz of the war, named Linebacker II, lasted nearly two weeks. Wide areas of the Hanoi-Haiphong industrial complex were left in flames and rubble.

Reports from Hanoi said as many as 2,000 persons were killed and another 2,000 wounded in what became known as Nixon's Christmas bombing campaign. A group of Americans who had just ended a visit to Hanoi said on their arrival in Hong Kong that the American raids had caused widespread damage to civilian areas and inflicted many civilian casualties. Joan Baez, the American folk singer, and other members of her group said the Bach Mai hospital and residential areas they had visited had been "completely destroyed" by bombs.

Another member of the group, Telford Taylor, of Columbia University, said, "Loss of life perhaps was not as high as might be expected considering the damage, but it has been very high in absolute terms, and the destruction has been terrible."

The aerial offensive also took an unprecedented toll in American Air Force losses. At least 27 American aircraft were shot down, including 15 B-52 bombers. Ninety-three airmen were killed, captured or listed as missing. North Vietnam indicated that, of those missing, at least one-third had been captured. Roughly this number were presented at a news conference and identified by name. The magnitude of the American losses was underscored by the fact that the 93 airmen lost in less than two weeks represented 21 percent of the 431 Americans known to have been captured by North Vietnam during the eight previous years.

Air Force Captain Roger Locher, a 28-year-old F-4 Phantom pilot from

The F-4 Phantom served as the workhorse of the Vietnam air war used by the Marines (top), the Air Force (middle) and the Navy (bottom). Capable of reaching speeds in excess of 1,600 MPH and able to carry more than 16,000 pounds of air munitions, the F-4 functioned as a reconnaissance craft, fighter-interceptor, fighter bomber and anything else required of it. Right: An F-4 swoops in for a bombing run against the communist positions near a Marine base at Nui Ba Ho just south of the DMZ.

During the first of two signing ceremonies, South Vietnamese Foreign Minister Tran Van Lam signs the peace agreement.

"It was a miracle," he said. "It's great to be back."

On December 30, President Nixon announced a halt to the bombing and the resumption of the Paris peace talks.

At 12:30 p.m. on January 27, 1973, the United States and North Vietnam signed the Paris peace agreement that ended direct American military involvement in Vietnam. President Nixon hailed the agreement as "peace with honor in Vietnam."

At the historic moment of the signing in the former Majestic Hotel in Paris, the ballroom crackled with hostility between Saigon's foreign minister, Tran Van Lam, and the North Vietnamese and Viet Cong delegations.

Secretary of State William P. Rogers signed his name 62 times to the various documents and protocols on behalf of the United States. America's longest war was over. Its 562 prisoners of war would come home.

U.S. Secretary of State William Rogers signs the agreement. Below: *The signatures of the four parties to the agreement. Top, U.S. Secretary of State William Rogers; below that, South Vietnamese Minister of Foreign Affairs Tran Van Lam; below that, Nguyen Thi Binh for the People's Revolutionary Government (VC); and finally, North Vietnam's Minister for Foreign Affairs Nguyen Duy Trinh.*

Sabetha, Kansas, might well have been among the prisoners. However, through his stealth and resourcefulness, he avoided an invitation to the "Hanoi Hilton," a prisoner of war camp for downed American pilots located in the North Vietnamese capital. On his 407th combat mission, his jet was hit by a missile from a Soviet-built MIG interceptor after he had shot down his third MIG in three months. The F-4 went out of control, flopping from side to side.

"Fire started coming in the back of the cockpit," he said. "It seared my canopy with bubbles, and I couldn't see out anymore. The airplane slowed down, and we went into a flat spin. I yanked for what seemed like an eternity on my primary ejection. The next thing I heard was a big blast. When I opened my eyes, I was in my parachute, and just about then I could see the airplane hit the ground right below. I looked around and was going into a kind of deep-dished valley. I aimed for a steep mountainside and came down through the trees. My heels were on the ground, so all I could do was unbuckle and get out. I just sat down for a minute and listened."

For the next 23 days, Locher sneaked through Hanoi's backyard, unable to make contact with American bombers flying overhead each day on their way to and from bombing strikes against North Vietnam. Locher kept on the move, hiking as much as 15 miles a day to find a secure position. On occasion, NVA soldiers passed within 20 feet of the downed airman, but his camouflage protected him. He lived on fruits, nuts and berries. At one point in his lonely trek, he got so bored that he shaved twice in one day with a surgical knife from his survival kit "just for the hell of it."

"One day," he said, "I eyed a banana tree all day. It didn't have any bananas on it, but I remembered I could get water out of it. Just before evening I stuck a hole in it and got myself three pints of good banana water. On another day, I went through somebody's garden and stole some chives. In this one clearing there was a hootch, and behind it was a pretty steep little mountain, so I just clambered right up their garden and halfway up their mountain quite near the top. That's where I stayed the last two days."

Although he could hear the American fighter-bombers passing overhead, and also the North Vietnamese firing at them, Locher was unable to contact them. Finally, two flights heard the beeper signal from his pocket radio and answered. An Air Force armada of up to 40 fighters and helicopters, driven off once by MIGs, returned to pluck him from his mountainside perch.

161

CHAPTER 13
FREE AT LAST

January 29, 1973. Going home.

At last, the doors would open, at the Hanoi Hilton, the Zoo Annex and all the other North Vietnamese prisons where American servicemen had endured as much as 8½ years under sometimes brutal conditions. Two days earlier, in Paris, U.S. and North Vietnamese representatives had signed a peace agreement freeing the POWs. Now was a time for rejoicing.

Above: *The joy of freedom fills the faces of Lieutenant Commander Gareth L. Anderson of Kane, Pennsylvania (left), and Lieutenant Commander Read B. Mecleary of Old Greenwich, Connecticut.*

At the Hanoi Hilton, however, there were no shouts of joy, no backslapping among the Americans as the hated commandant, nicknamed Weasel by the prisoners, impassively informed them that they were to be released. Many simply were numb and gaunt, having lost a third of their weight on the meager diet ordered by the North Vietnamese commandant. Some had broken legs and arms that had not been set. Others did not want to be used in a propaganda event, fearing that communist cameras might be recording their emotions. Not a few remembered the hundreds of other Americans for whom there would be no homecoming, having died in captivity from lack of medical attention, starvation and the brutality of the camps.

"Ten good men died in my arms, and I'm damned mad about that," said Army Major Floyd Kushner, a physician who was a prisoner initially held in South

Home at last. His family rushing to greet him, Lieutenant Colonel Robert L. Stirm lands at Travis Air Force Base after being released by the North Vietnamese in 1973. The tales of torture which many of the returning POWs brought with them out of captivity shocked America. (Pulitzer Prize photo by Sal Veder, 1973.)

163

For the first time in eight years the doors to the Hanoi Hilton stand open. Two days earlier, 33 Americans walked through these doors for the last time, finally returning to the United States.

Vietnam. "It was all the result of maltreatment in South Vietnam. Our mortality rate in South Vietnam [among POWs] was 45 percent. I guess there was a parallel with Japanese treatment during World War II."

Major John Dramesi, a 40-year-old Air Force pilot from Blackwood, New Jersey, who escaped twice from North Vietnamese prisons, said he believed a fellow escapee, Major Edwin Atter-berry, of Dallas, Texas, was tortured and fatally beaten after they had broken out of the Zoo Annex prison in Hanoi. Dramesi recalled being beaten and tortured for 30 days after he was recaptured.

In order to extract propaganda statements from Colonel Robinson Risner of Oklahoma City, North Vietnamese jailers attached 60-pound bars to his ankles and trussed him with ropes. As the iron bars pressed for hours against his ankles, the pain slowly rose until it reached an excruciating level. Risner agreed to make the statements.

"I made more than one tape," said the 48-year-old Risner. "I wrote what they told me to write after a torture session. If I was told to say the war was wrong, I said the war was wrong ... The pain became too severe. I myself have screamed all night. I have heard as many as four people holler at one time."

Prisoners were also tortured with rope devices used to inflict pain and cut off circulation of their blood. Others were made to kneel on hard floors for hours at a time and kept in isolation for years, forced to sit in their own filth. The North Vietnamese would even deny the prisoners needed medicine and medical attention.

Air Force Captain Joseph Milligan, of Annandale, New Jersey, said the only treatment he received for burns of the face and arms he suffered when he was shot down was a swabbing with hot water twice a week.

"They were draining quite badly," he said. "They were full of pus. They smelled rotten. One day I noticed some flies flying around my arms. I allowed them to land and lay eggs on my wounds. When the maggots hatched, they ate the dead flesh. After the dead flesh was gone, I went over to the buckets in my cell. I urinated over my arms to wash the maggots off, tore up a tee shirt, and rewrapped my arms. And after that they healed."

Navy Lieutenant Commander John McCain III, 36, shot down and captured in October, 1967, said the North Vietnamese both saved his life and tortured him after they learned his father was an admiral who would command the United States forces in the Pacific.

"My leg was broken, and I had other injuries when I was shot down," he said. "After four days with no medical treatment whatever ... I realized I was dying .... The Bug [the North Vietnamese jailer] came in and brought a doctor. I asked, 'Are you going to take me to the hospital?' And they said, 'Too late, too late.'"

The Bug returned a short time later and told McCain, "Your father is a big admiral." McCain was then sent to the hospital, where he was treated.

"In mid-1968, a man in charge of all the camps tried to get me to accept release," McCain said. "I didn't know at the time that it coincided with my father's appointment as commander in the Pacific. When I refused to take release ahead of Commander Everett Alvarez and the others who had been there longer, the treatment became very bad."

McCain's leg was rebroken, one arm

was broken, his teeth were smashed, and other injuries were inflicted in torture sessions.

"In 1970 I was told I would see some of 'our foreign guests,' as they called them," McCain said. "I refused to do so, and I was taken to a room we called Calcutta. I spent the summer in a 6-by-2-foot room with a 6-by-2-inch window."

Navy Captain Jeremiah Denton, Jr., 48, of Virginia Beach, Virginia, said that beginning in October, 1965, the

Left: *The empty living quarters of American POWs in the Hanoi Hilton. Personal possessions amassed during the years of captivity lie forgotten on the prison floor.* Below: *North Vietnamese guards peruse magazines and notebooks left behind at the Hanoi Hilton. The fortress like prison was built in the late nineteenth century by the French.*

Nine U.S. military and civilian personnel held captive by the Laotian communists are transported to Gia Lam Airport in Hanoi where they were turned over to U.S. officials.

North Vietnamese tried by torture and isolation to steamroller all of the POWs into tools of anti-Americanism and antiwar propaganda.

"They failed," he said. "Determined men can defeat a system of torture purges such as the North Vietnamese imposed on American prisoners prior to December, 1966. Our only effective weapon against the system was for the whole group to resist exploitation to the point at which they were tortured beyond the will to resist, finally causing the North Vietnamese to see there was no expediency in torturing us en masse anymore. As a result of our hard-line resistance in 1966, they were deterred from continuing with all the objectives of en masse subjugation. That was the year we prisoners achieved unity and became of age."

Denton's jet had been hit in July, 1965 while leading a raid of 28 aircraft against the port facility of Thanh Hoa. He and his navigator-bombardier, Commander William Tschudy, bailed out when the plane lost power.

"When we came out, I thought we had a good chance to evade [capture], since we were in a relatively unpopulated area," he said. Struggling to keep his wildly swinging parachute from collapsing, he did not yet notice the injury to his left leg.

"I was amazed at the volume of small arms and automatic weapons fire, and I kind of got the feeling they might be shooting at us," he said.

"The wind blew us back over the river and then, instead of continuing to blow us across the river north to a spot where we might have a chance to evade, it changed course at the river and blew us westward right back toward the bridge in the target area. I saw that I was going to land in the river and there were soldiers on the south bank in great droves. . . . When I did surface, I found soldiers just standing there with their guns, pointing at me.

" . . . I remember stopping at huts where the people were not antagonistic. One woman seemed to be angry, but the other people weren't. On two occasions at huts, I was given tea and coconut milk for strength. They put me on display in a political hall, and as they filed through, their faces were sympathetic."

When North Vietnamese efforts to break the whole group of POWs were at their height, Denton was placed in rig irons with his legs crossed, his left wrist tightly handcuffed to the iron bar.

"By morning, each of my lower legs looked like a swollen football with a POW bracelet around the middle of the swelling. I'd lost most of the feeling in my legs, but the pain was getting worse in my normally bad back and in my lower legs. I didn't scream. I was just too weak.

"I would have signaled that I'd write a statement they wanted, but I knew they would have left me there anyway. It was really punishment with the aim of subjugation and punishment for ruining the press conferences—not coercion for some statement. They already had a 'confession' and they knew I'd die before giving them any useful

166

Four U.S. POWs are returned to a detention center in Hanoi after refusing invitations from the Joint Military Commission to be interviewed. The last POWs were released on March 29.

A fellow POW talks with several others placed in detention in Hanoi.

information. But before letting me out, they got me to agree to write a new statement and something 'military.' The statements were bad—about leading my pilots many times to bomb churches, schools and hospitals. But the 'military' statement was harmless drivel."

Of the more than 7½ years Denton was held captive, four were spent in solitary confinement. As with many of the other prisoners, he found the isolation and loneliness as difficult to handle as any of the physical torture.

"A man does a lot of thinking during seven years, seven months in enemy prisons," he said. "Mental exercise... helped the mind escape the confines of tiny cells. But even more than thinking, a man does a lot of praying in an enemy prison. Prayer, even more than sheer thought, is the firmest anchor to windward."

Many of the prisoners turned to prayer, even those who had strayed from the church over the years. Although the Weasel only allowed the

A U.S. pilot surrenders to North Vietnamese militia after bailing out over North Vietnam.

captives to use the Bible on special religious holidays, they managed to make it an integral part of their lives. Major Norman McDaniel, of Greensboro, North Carolina, and other prisoners memorized as much of the book as possible during religious holidays, then wrote down what they remembered when they were allowed pencil and paper.

U.S. POWs engage in a game of basketball inside a North Vietnamese prison.

America rejoiced when the POWs returned home, beginning in February.

Navy Commander Brian Woods, of San Diego, California, and Air Force Major Glendon Perkins, of Orlando, Florida, the first two of the returning prisoners, stepped onto their native soil in San Diego with a salute.

"This homecoming is not only for myself and Glendon Perkins, but for all the POWs," Woods said. "We are grateful and overwhelmed."

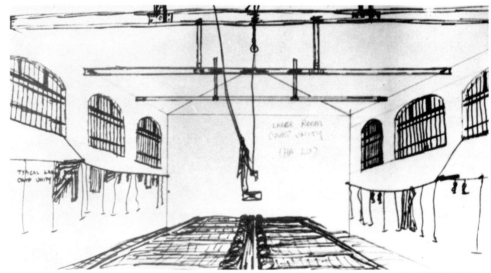

Sketch of a large room at Camp Unity, Ha Lo Prison in Hanoi, by POW Navy Commander Charles N. Tanner. Tanner later detailed some of the tortures he endured as a prisoner. Below: Traffic passes by the outside wall of the Hanoi Hilton.

Model of the Son Tay Prison prepared by the Defense Department.

SON TAY

2:00 a.m. Saturday, November 21, 1970. Only a quarter moon broke the dark night over Vietnam. In jungle fatigues, their faces blackened to meld into the darkness, some 40 men sped in helicopters across the North Vietnamese delta to a compound at the town of Son Tay, on the Red River 23 miles west of Hanoi, the communist capital.

All these men were volunteers, dedicated, specially trained Army and Air Force personnel with one goal in mind: to free the American prisoners of war at the Son Tay camp. They had been trained for that purpose since August on mockups at Fort Bragg in North Carolina, Eglin Air Force Base in Florida and at several other secret locations. Their wives and families believed they were on routine field maneuvers. Although they had exchanged letters with their families, the military had arranged for the origins of the letters to be kept secret.

Ground leader for the Son Tay prison raid was Army Colonel Arthur Simons, 52, known as "The Bull." Simons had led numerous elite assignments, starting with the Rangers in World War II and including the Special Forces' SOG (Studies and Operations Group) in Vietnam, which made regular raids into Laos, Cambodia and North Vietnam. In overall command of the Son Tay mission was Air Force Brigadier General Leroy J. Manor.

The final go-ahead for the daring mission was given early Friday morning, November 13, with President Nixon's full approval. One week later, the volunteer reserve group lifted off from a secret air base in northern Thailand, probably Nakhon Phanom, a top-secret installation 265 miles south-southwest of Hanoi. As they approached the compound, some 30 missiles were fired at the helicopters. One helicopter was purposely crashlanded on the prison grounds.

There was some ground fire as they landed. In the ensuing action, a watch-tower was destroyed. The volunteers fired their weapons sparingly as they swept through the prison compound, silencing several enemy positions. They did not waste time with a body count but continued steadily toward the prison cells. Only one member of the attack force was injured during the assault, nicked by an enemy rifle round.

For more than half an hour, the volunteers searched through the prison, ripping open cells with chain saws, torches and lock snips, finding crude prison conditions, but no American prisoners. All the evidence they found indicated that the prisoners had been moved two or three weeks earlier.

There was some domestic criticism of the unsuccessful raid. Some blamed an intelligence leak. Others, fearing retaliation, thought the failure only put American prisoners of war in greater jeopardy.

Secretary of Defense Laird felt differently. He characterized the raid as a signal to Hanoi "that we care about these men, and that we will take rather unusual means to see that these men are returned as free Americans." He said he recommended the raid because "our men were dying in captivity" and because American prisoners felt they had been forgotten.

"Many of our prisoners of war were losing their hope and their faith. We have not only shown North Vietnam, but we have shown the prisoners of war, that we do care, that we do have the capability to go forward with their rescue...

"I have no regrets about its being recommended. My only regret is that we did not bring out any prisoners of war, but that was a chance we had to take. It is my firm belief that if there had been prisoners of war at Son Tay, they would have been free men today."

One of the officers in the daring assault, 31-year-old Army First Lieutenant George W. Petrie of Lenoir, North Carolina, later said he and his companions in the attack felt "pretty bad" when they discovered the camp held no American prisoners.

"I expected to hear them hollering at us," he said. "But when there were no voices, I knew there was no one there."

He said the raid was sprung with clockwork efficiency and that there was no confusion on the ground.

He added, "I'd do it again tomorrow if I had the chance."

Henry Kissinger and North Vietnamese Politburo member Le Duc Tho sit across from each other as they initial the Vietnam Peace Agreement in Paris on January 24, 1973. The two leaders were awarded the Nobel peace prize for their efforts at reaching the agreement. Below: Folksinger Joan Baez (right) and Columbia University law professor Telford Taylor describe what they had seen in Hanoi following the U.S. bombing offensive. Taylor described many sections of the city as "shattered and virtually erased."

Perkins was shot down over North Vietnam in 1966 when his son was three years old.

"Hi, Daddy," his son had said earlier over the phone before Perkins arrived in San Diego, "I love you. This is Michael. I'm seven now."

Navy Lieutenant Commander Edward Davis, of Leola, Pennsylvania, brought home with him a puppy named Ma-co, Vietnamese for "dog with no hair." He had adopted the puppy during his confinement.

Everett Alvarez, the first American flyer shot down in Vietnam, who was held prisoner 8½ years, appeared gaunt and unsmiling. He was now 35 years old.

"For years and years we've dreamed of this day and we kept faith—faith in

March 28, 1973. USAF Captain William R. Schwertfeger of Caldwell, Kansas, is welcomed upon his release at Gia Lam Airport. Schwertfeger was in the last group of prisoners released.

God, in our president and our country. . . . We have many things to be thankful for here. We have many things we consider commonplace. I missed these most of all . . . like the things you find around the house."

Alvarez had been married only two months when he left in 1964 for a tour of duty on the aircraft carrier USS *Constellation*. But it would be a bittersweet homecoming. His wife, Tangee, had divorced him two years earlier and remarried.

"I just hope he understands," she said. "I didn't plan what happened between us. I loved him a lot at one time and I am very proud to have once been his wife. But the main thing now is he is home safely and free at last."

Left: *Marine Sergeant Ronald L. Ridgeway heads toward U.S. evacuation plane at Gia Lam Airport. Reported killed at Khe Sanh in 1968, Ridgeway showed up five years later as a prisoner in North Vietnam.* Above: *At his inaugural address on January 20, President Nixon stated that the world "stands on the threshold of a new era of peace." However, although the United States had finally withdrawn its troops from Vietnam, the war there would continue for two more years.* Following pages: *Jubilation fills the cabin as the C-141 transport lifts off from Gia Lam Airport in Hanoi carrying these 108 POWs on the first leg of their journey home.*

171

CHAPTER 14
THE EXODUS

The last 23,000 American troops in Vietnam went home in February and March of 1973. The American mission in Vietnam, which once had included more than half a million troops and several thousand civilians, now consisted of 50 military attaches and 1,200 civilians at the Defense Attache Office at the Pentagon East in Tan Son Nhut Air Base and another 150 Marines at the U.S. Embassy.

Despite the departure of U.S. combat forces, the war continued unabated in the two years following the signing of the Paris agreement as the North Vietnamese and the Viet Cong launched a series of limited regional offensives. The communist command now concentrated on consolidating its areas of control, mainly in the underpopulated border regions, and on improving a new road network supplementing the Ho Chi Minh trail through southern Laos.

The two-party Joint Military Commission, consisting of representatives of the Saigon government and the Viet Cong, which had been assigned the task of enforcing the cease-fire, made no effort to stop the fighting. Instead, each side used the commission as a propaganda forum. The four-nation International Commission for Control and Supervision (ICCS) proved equally ineffective in supervising the Paris agreement. Split along political lines, with Indonesia and Iran backing the United States and Saigon, and Poland and Hungary supporting the communists, the commission lacked the solidarity necessary to carry out its task.

During the first two years of "peace," official Saigon figures showed more than 26,000 government troops killed, more than 108,000 wounded, and another 15,000 missing. The Saigon command also claimed that more than 100,000 North Vietnamese and Viet Cong had been killed since the Paris agreement. Thousands of civilians were killed, wounded or left homeless, and the number of refugees grew to 10 million, more than half of South Vietnam's entire population.

By early 1975, the outlook for the South Vietnamese appeared bleak. Morale within the army had seriously deteriorated as a result of mounting casualties, corruption within the officer corps and dwindling U.S. aid. In the first quarter of 1975 alone, 59,862 men deserted from the South Vietnamese

Carrying his baby brother on his back, a Vietnamese boy flees with his family from the Central Highland city of Pleiku.

175

Above: *The tranquility of this scene from Tay Ninh Province belies the growing seriousness of the situation. Within four months the province would be under the control of the communists.* Below: *South Vietnamese troops turn in their weapons at Long Hai after fleeing the Central Highlands.*

armed forces. At the same time, communist forces were again taking the offensive.

A Fateful Decision

The final collapse began on March 11. In a battle lasting just over 24 hours, North Vietnamese forces routed Saigon troops from the city of Ban Me Thuot, the southern anchor of Saigon's defenses in the Central Highlands. That same day, the U.S. House of Representatives rejected President Ford's $300 million supplementary military aid bill for South Vietnam, and it appeared unlikely that any more aid would be approved in the next U.S. budget in July.

Confronted by a larger, better equipped foe, and facing the prospect of an imminent shutdown of U.S. military aid, Thieu was forced to make a dramatic decision. On March 14, he called together several of his top military advisers at Cam Ranh Bay to reveal his new plan. The sparsely populated Highlands, he declared, always an economic and military liability for the Saigon

Above: *East of Ban Me Thout, Vietnamese refugees flee on foot down Highway 21. The Central Highland city fell to communist forces after a short one day battle.* Below: *Vietnamese refugees jam the docks in Da Nang harbor as the North Vietnamese forces close in the city.*

government, must be abandoned. All government forces would now be withdrawn to the larger, more easily defended, coastal cities. The withdrawal would begin at once with the immediate evacuation of Pleiku and Kontum.

U.S. military leaders had long urged Thieu to adopt such an enclave strategy. However, when the South Vietnamese leader finally opted in its favor, he did so out of expediency without thorough planning. As a result, what might have been an orderly retreat quickly turned into a rout.

By the evening of March 15, thousands of soldiers and civilians clogged the roads leading eastward to the coast. Those fortunate enough to have cars or trucks loaded them with their mattresses, furniture and kitchen utensils. When any car or truck stalled, tanks leading the 20-mile long column of 4,000 vehicles simply rolled over them or shoved them off to the side of the road. "This is the fourth time I have run from the communists," said an elderly storekeeper from Pleiku at the start of the evacuation. "I really don't know where there is a safe place to hide."

Nguyen Tu, a South Vietnamese newsman in Pleiku at the time, witnessed the tragic exodus from the highlands.

"Many thousands . . . trudged along the roads, burned by the sun during the day, chilled by the cold of the jungle at night," he reported. "Thousands of military and civilian vehicles moved bumper to bumper down Highway 14. Drivers and motorcyclists, overanxious to escape, caused a traffic jam several miles long.

"Along the road, children collapsed, fathers and mothers wept at their children's thirst and hunger. As the refugees entered Cheo Reo (the capital of Phu Bon province), the townspeople joined them. Men, women and children poured into the streets with what they could carry, and ran. Then the looting began. Several groups of buildings were [set] on fire. Phu Bon was falling by itself."

Once outside of Cheo Reo, now on Highway 7, the refugees ran into increasing harassment from the North Vietnamese and Viet Cong. Near the

overloading the aircraft. Eventually, South Vietnamese rangers assumed control of the situation, organizing the people into groups of 16 to 20.

At Tuy Hoa, the refugees, fatigued and sick, many of them weeping, stumbled out of the helicopters. Some carried a few personal possessions, others only the clothes on their backs.

One old woman, on the road for seven days, dropped down on the ground near the helicopter pad, crying, "Now I know I am alive!" Two schoolchildren arrived alone. Their father had placed them aboard mistakenly believing that their pregnant mother had gotten on before them. A schoolteacher told how he had traveled with his family through the jungle to avoid artillery fire and believed that their luck had changed for the better when they were picked up by a truck, only to find that their five-year-old son had been lost in the scramble.

"It was everyone for himself," said a woman from Kontum. "We started in a car with several other people, and we bought gasoline from straggling soldiers. Then when our car broke down we marched by day and night through

Tuy Hoa with her children, but without her husband, from whom she had been separated during the first shelling, summed up the evacuation march. "It was such misery I cannot describe it."

Many members of the military were upset at the orders to abandon Pleiku and Kontum without a fight. "We are running without a fight," complained a young ARVN private. "This is so humiliating. At least we should have a fight before running." Lieutenant Dang Van Ba, a helicopter pilot, echoed the soldier's sentiments. "We are still fighting, and we haven't been defeated, so why should we run?" His commander, Captain Tran Dinh Toan, was more subdued with his criticism. "This is all so sad. When we looked back at Pleiku there was nothing left except the fire. I felt so distressed." One Vietnamese ranger spoke for many of his fellow soldiers when he said, "I really can't face the people this time."

Even North Vietnam was surprised by South Vietnam's retreat from the Central Highlands. The north's generals had planned only a series of attacks to soften up the south for a general offensive in 1976 whose objective would be complete victory.

"Why such a retreat?" asked General Van Tien Dung, North Vietnam's chief of staff. "And who had given the order for it? Was it true that the thunderous blow we had dealt at Ban Me Thuot had produced such a shattering impact on the enemy? It was true that the enemy had been stunned and rendered strategically confused. The enemy had again made another grave strategic mistake. . . . "

The Final Collapse

The retreat from the Highlands triggered another wave of panic across South Vietnam. The northern provinces fell next, including Hue and Da Nang, South Vietnam's second-largest city. The central coast cities of Nha Trang and Phan Rang were abandoned without a fight as South Vietnamese deserted by the hundreds. Meanwhile, President Thieu had retreated to the isolation of Independence Palace, where aides brought him reports of the growing list of reverses upon the battlefield.

On March 25, the city of Hue fell. Peter Arnett, an Associated Press special correspondent, compared the evacuation of tens of thousands of Vietnamese soldiers and civilian refugees from the ancient capital to the British evacuation of Dunkirk in World War II. As the North Vietnamese approached, troops of the South Vietnamese 1st Division fled with their families down the 10-mile highway to Thuan An beach, where an ocean of

Above: *A South Vietnamese girl carries her younger brother to a waiting helicopter near Tuy Hoa on South Vietnam's central coast.* Right: *April 1. A South Vietnamese Marine comforts his wife aboard a South Vietnamese LST in Da Nang harbor.*

village of Cung Son, a reported 100 persons, mostly civilians, were killed by communist shelling. Finally, after eight days of travel, the column was trapped only 15 miles from the coastal city of Tuy Hoa and safety.

A helicopter evacuation was initiated to rescue the stranded refugees. At first, panic and disorder marred the evacuation as up to 30 refugees crammed onto each helicopter, seriously

the jungle trails [and] bought water from Montagnard villagers. We were near death several times. Once, the military police had a battle with the rangers [apparently over position in the evacuation column]. There were many deaths, but I don't know how many. We are very happy to be here. We have no car, but we are alive and can work to buy another car."

One mother who had safely reached

Above: *Human cargo. Refugees are dropped onto the deck of an already jammed evacuation ship by a cargo sling off Thuan An beach.* Below left: *Refugees from the ancient city of Hue ride a motley assortment of vehicles fleeing south through the Hai Van Pass as North Vietnamese forces push toward the ancient city.* Below right: *The losers in every war. A small Vietnamese carries her young brother to safety near Tuy Hoa.*

Above: *A Vietnamese driver, with his family and belongings piled onto his pedicab, flees Hue as communist forces approach the city. More than 80 percent of the city's 200,000 residents fled before the communists took control.* Below: *Aboard a U.S. C-46 helicopter, a Vietnamese girl cradles her baby brother in her arms.*

people waited for evacuation. Some of the soldiers ripped off their boots and trousers, tossed away their rifles, and plunged into the light surf, swimming 500 yards to Navy ships and civilian vessels standing off the coast. American military equipment estimated to be worth $100 million lay strewn behind them, transforming the Hue estuary into a giant military junkyard.

In Da Nang, the streets were jammed with refugees from Hue and other cities, tripling the city's population of 500,000. Food and other essentials soon became scarce. Refugees who had lived there for years complained that no rice had reached them for 10 days. Banks limited withdrawals to 20 percent of deposits, nearly touching off mass riots. Finally, as the North Vietnamese drew near, residents and soldiers embarked on a three-day rampage of looting, burning and murder.

Frightened soldiers, civil servants and civilians rushed to the Da Nang airport and waterfront to escape. At the Da Nang airport, American secur-

Members of a beaten army. Weary South Vietnamese Marines crowd the deck of an LST evacuation ship in Da Nang Harbor.

ity men fired shots into the air to drive back panicky Vietnamese who broke through barriers to try to board refugee flights, heading off a stampede. However, as the last flight, a World Airways 727, prepared to leave, some 5,000 Vietnamese broke through and stormed across the tarmac toward the plane. Vietnamese soldiers shoved women and children aside in their attempts to board the plane. In their desperation, several soldiers damaged the plane with grenades as they attempted to clear the way. Even as the plane rumbled down the runway for takeoff, many Vietnamese clung to the landing gear. Several were crushed to

181

Panicky South Vietnamese Marines clamber aboard a cutter from an LST in Da Nang harbor.

Part of a motley fleet of private, commercial and naval vessels assembled by the South Vietnamese government to evacuate the retreating South Vietnamese army.

Refugees crowd aboard the evacuation ship Pioneer Contender *south of Da Dang.* Above right: *Cargo nets lift refugees onto the deck of the* Pioneer Contender.

death when the gear was retracted into the plane following takeoff.

At Da Nang harbor, Associated Press correspondent Peter O'Loughlin, aboard the refugee ship *Pioneer Contender*, reported scenes of panic and fear in the last, violent scramble for space aboard ships and barges. Refugees jammed every conceivable section of the crafts. Many crowded into cargo nets like cattle, with many more clinging to the outside of the nets. In the tremendous press of humanity, several babies fell into the water, followed by their mothers leaping to save them. One woman's baby died in her arms as she waited on a barge along with 6,000 other refugees for four days without food, water, shelter or toilet facilities. When she finally got the chance to board the *Pioneer Contender*, she became hysterical and leapt overboard. Those who survived on the barge looted the possessions of those who had died.

April 25. Private First Class Joseph Johnson of Jetersville, Virginia, carries a Vietnamese baby during evacuation operations. Johnson, a member of the 1st Battalion, 4th Marine Division, was part of a security force assigned to protect the evacuation ships.

Vietnamese, Americans and other foreigners during the first week of April.

An Air Force C-5A transport took off on April 4 with 226 Vietnamese orphans, most of them babies strapped two to a seat, to begin Operation Babylift, a highly publicized evacuation of 2,000 orphans. Also aboard were 77 Americans, including the crew and other servicemen and civilians escorting the orphans to their new homes in the United States, Canada and Europe.

Fifteen minutes after takeoff, a lock system failed and doors blew off at 23,000 feet. Oxygen masks dropped,

Marauding South Vietnamese troops fought sea battles to take over lighters (small freighters) and barges that could take them to the *Pioneer Contender* and its sister ship, the *Pioneer Commander*. One group of South Vietnamese Marines shot and killed 25 refugees clinging to the fantail of the *Pioneer Commander*, claiming they were VC.

When the *Pioneer Contender* finally left on March 30, the last ship to depart before the North Vietnamese captured the city, an estimated 100,000 had been evacuated. However, another 1.4 million remained behind, and hundreds more had either drowned or died of exposure trying to escape.

By mid-April, nearly half of South Vietnam's 44 provinces were in the hands of the North Vietnamese and Viet Cong, representing three-fourths of the country's land and one-half of its 20 million people. The United States had already begun evacuating some

USAF crewmen from a C-141 carry four of a group of 90 South Vietnamese orphans to their aircraft. The children were taken to the United States for adoption.

183

April 28. A South Vietnamese tank retreats toward Saigon down Route 15 as communist troops closed in on the South Vietnamese capital.

but there weren't enough to go around. The escorts ran through the aisles switching masks from child to child. The pilot turned back and made a crash landing in a rice paddy near Saigon.

April 5. South Vietnamese President Nguyen Van Thieu announces his resignation from the government. Facing page: *A civilian American pilot struggles to control panicking Vietnamese civilians as they crowd onto his plane in the coastal city of Nha Trang on April 1.*

184

More than 75 orphans died, 50 Americans were killed, and 27 were injured.

The South Vietnamese forces finally withdrew to the Saigon area to make a final stand at Xuan Loc, a small pro-vincial capital 35 miles east.

President Thieu pledged that troops of the crack 18th Infantry Division, reinforced by an elite paratrooper regiment, would defend Saigon until death.

"We will fight to the last bullet, the last grain of rice," he said.

The Saigon forces did stand and fight at Xuan Loc but took heavy losses. It was becoming clear they could not hold the line. Even now, more North Vietnamese convoys were moving southward to reinforce elements of 12 divisions already within easy striking distance of Saigon with heavy artillery.

With South Vietnam falling apart, President Thieu resigned on April 21 and flew to Taipei in an 11th-hour bid for a political settlement, bowing to Viet Cong demands for his ouster as a first step toward talks.

In a tearful address, Thieu bitterly accused the United States of moves he claimed "led the South Vietnamese people to death." He said the United States had broken a promise to come to South Vietnam's defense in case of a major violation of the 1973 peace accords.

Following Thieu's resignation, most of Saigon's top military officers, including Lieutenant General Nguyen Van Minh, commander of the capital's military defenses, fled the country.

The end was near.

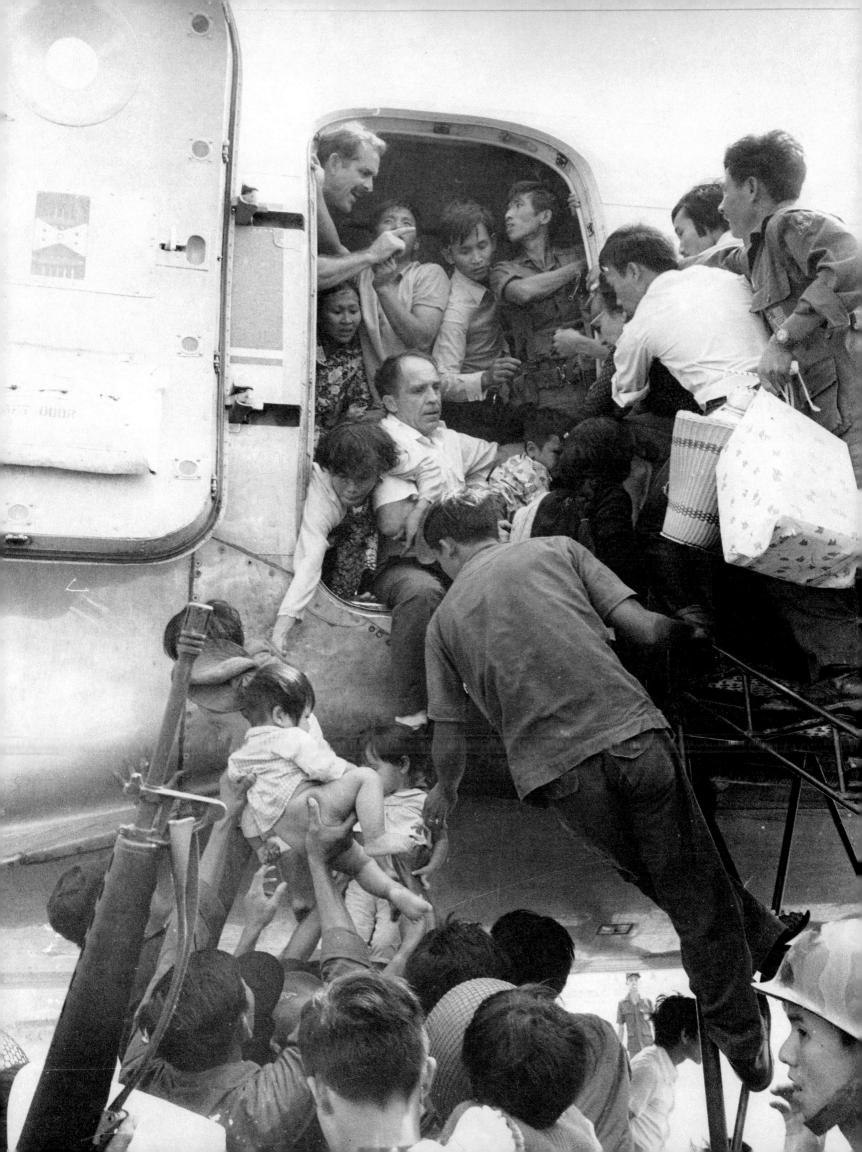

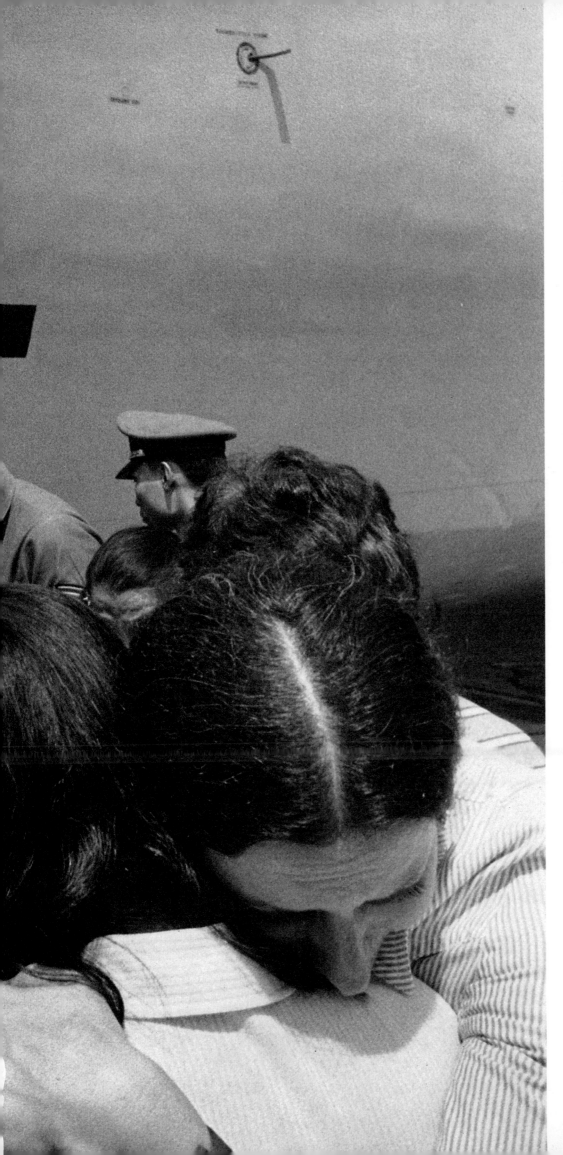

CHAPTER 15
THE FINAL EVACUATION

Saigon. April 29 dawned with a rain of rockets and artillery shells. For more than three hours, from 4:10 a.m. until 7:15, North Vietnamese gunners relentlessly poured shellfire onto Tan Son Nhut Air Base. Marine Corporals Charles McMahon Jr., 21, of Woburn, Massachusetts, and Darwin Judge, 19, of Marshalltown, Iowa, were standing guard there when the first rounds struck. Both had arrived in Vietnam only recently. Three weeks earlier, Judge had written to his mother telling her that she would be hearing from him frequently because "at night there isn't much else to do when you're standing post." Neither he nor McMahon would survive the early morning shelling. They would be the last Americans to die in Vietnam.

The attack hastened orders from Washington to pull out the remaining 1,000 Americans and as many Vietnamese as possible who were thought to be marked for death by the communists.

With American fighter planes flying cover, evacuation helicopters from U.S. carriers in the South China Sea swarmed over Saigon, landing on the roofs at the U.S. Embassy and at Tan Son Nhut Air Base.

Outside the embassy compound, hundreds of Vietnamese tried to claw their way over the 14-foot wall surrounding the compound in desperate attempts to reach the American helicopters. Battle-garbed Marines and civilians beat the Vietnamese back with pistol and rifle butts, feet and fists.

AP correspondent Edwin Q. White and AP photographer Neal Ulevich stood outside the embassy with a group of 30 newsmen. Earlier, after reaching a prearranged marshaling point, White and the other newsmen had boarded a bus and driven around Saigon looking for a place to be picked up by U.S. helicopters. After being turned away at Tan Son Nhut and the docks, they had turned toward the embassy. Now they had to find a way through the crowds massed at the gate. Ulevich reported:

We knew the Marines would take us in. We had to get in close. Thousands of Vietnamese were at the wall, hoping to climb over and into a helicopter. The Marines

Actress Ina Balin (foreground) puts her arms around a Vietnamese mother whose child is being placed aboard an American C-141 for transportation to the U.S. where the baby will be adopted.

187

Hi Mom

How have you been it is beautiful weather here and I really like it here. The people are real nice here and in a lot of the places there are real neat flower gardens. Say hellow to everybody for me and that I should be writeing a lot because at night there isn't much else to do when you are standing post but some more money in my checking accat and then write and tell me how mucch because I haven't been paid since the 28th of Feb. You said that I would be able to afford all the stuff I wanted I have ordered my two pairs of glasses and they are both wire rims and the sun glass perscirtio cost $23.00 and the regular perscartioi cost $20.00. And there are harden lens and the best you can get. so that isn't too bad.

So fer, I really like it here and especialy the wether. So Don't worry about all the junk in the papers because its ture but I am all right and all the ether marines and me take care of each ether.

With Love,
Your Son.

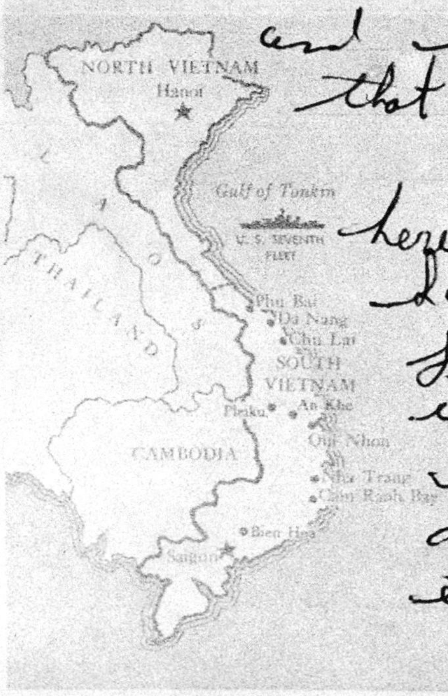

Lance Corporal Darwin Judge's letter home. On April 28 "all that junk in the papers" finally caught up with the young Marine who died on the final day of the evacuation.

188

Telegram

3/2 BBF 227 San Francisco

Mr & Mrs Charles McMahon
51 Montvale Ave
Woburn

Remains of your son, Cpl. Charles McMahon Jr.
are schuled to depart San Fran. Calif via Am Air lines
flgt. 160 March 2 1976 at 11:55 p.m. arrive Boston
10:40 AM March 3rd. Everett Behby + son Funeral Home
has been requested to meet plane. Escort S/msgt
Francis McMahon will accompany remains.
Sincerest Sympathy extended.

Signed
Commanding Off.
Naval Dispensary
Treasure Island
San Francisco Calif

WU 1201 (R 5-69)

Western Union telegram informs the parents of Charles McMahon that their son's body will arrive home on March 2, 1976, nearly one year after his death.

Above left: *Flanked by the twin spires of the Saigon Cathedral, a U.S. Marine helicopter heads for the U.S. Embassy to evacuate another group of refugees.* Above right: *Americans and Vietnamese stand outside the U.S. Embassy awaiting evacuation.* Below: *Desperate Vietnamese struggle to scale the wall of the U.S. Embassy in Saigon in order to reach U.S. evacuation helicopters inside the compound.*

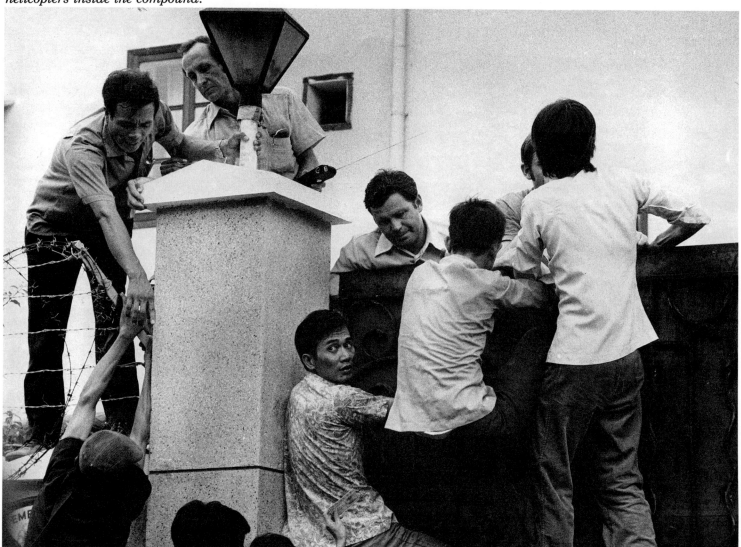

Above: April 18. Lines outside the consulate lengthen as the communists approach. Below: As the military situation deteriorated, Americans living and working in Saigon and their Vietnamese dependents traveled to the U.S. consul seeking exit visas and evacuation.

were pushing them back to keep the embassy from being overrun, allowing only Westerners and a few Saigon officials inside.

Vietnamese began to crawl over the barbed wire on top of the wall, like commandos. One man caught his leg and fell. He dangled upside down, hanging by a lacerated leg.

The Marines spotted us. Our group pushed nearer the wall. The crowd pressed closer. A youngster, perhaps 18, and half-American, clung desperately to my neck. "I will die if I stay," she cried out.

Mothers held their children above the mass of people for Marines to take them inside. One of my cameras disappeared. Then my watch was gone. The Marines, still kicking Vietnamese, started grabbing the Westerners by their collars and hauling them up.

[Once inside] it was easy. The embassy compound was in chaos, but a quiet man with a .45-caliber pistol in his belt led us to the inner court where Marines in combat gear guarded the walls.

He led us into the building to make our way to the roof. Waiting in the corridors, we saw men calmly destroying code machines with hammers. The place was littered. Offices now were deserted.

Telephones were ringing and no one was answering them.

We were nearing the end.

We heard the roar of the helicopter settling down on the embassy roof and we climbed the staircase. The Marine CH-46 was waiting when we emerged, its twin rotors turning great arcs in the drizzly grayness. Suddenly we were airborne and the lights of Saigon seemed like gems growing dimmer and smaller.

In a while, more lights, red gems this time: the deck lights of the USS *Okinawa*. We were down. We were safe.

All over Saigon, people sought ways to leave the country. Several South Vietnamese government officials came to the office of the Associated Press or telephoned to ask if they could be evacuated. Other Vietnamese stuck close to American reporters, thinking they would be their ticket out. One woman slept outside the apartment door of a reporter, not letting him out of her sight and wrongly assuming he would be evacuated.

At the entrance to Tan Son Nhut Air Base, abandoned American cars and

Top left: *As a North Vietnamese mortar round explodes on Newport Bridge on the outskirts of Saigon on April 28, U.S. newsmen and South Vietnamese troops run for cover.* Top right: *With embassy staff and U.S. Marines standing guard, a helicopter sits atop the U.S. Embassy awaiting passengers to take to U.S. ships standing off the coast.* Right: *Mobs of Vietnamese attempt to scale the wall of the U.S. Embassy. AP photographer Neal Ulevich, who took this photograph, barely succeeding in reaching the helicopter evacuation pad inside the Embassy.*

192

motorcycles littered the road. Many American evacuees had been turned back at the gates by resentful Vietnamese guards, firing into the air and shouting, "We want to go, too."

Across the street from the U.S. Embassy, Vietnamese soldiers, police and youths stole and stripped scores of abandoned embassy cars. Others looted apartment buildings in which Americans lived, taking bathroom fixtures, books, furniture, typewriters, air conditioners, radios, stereo equipment and food. They sat on the sidewalk with their booty, waiting for friends in cars to pick them up. The stolen goods turned up later on the black market where North Vietnamese soldiers would bargain with the Saigonese merchants at the sidewalk stalls.

The chaos reigning on the streets now was leaking over into the embassy. Colonel John H. Madison, Jr., chief of the U.S. delegation to the Four-Party Joint Military Team that helped carry out the provisions of the Paris peace agreement, described the situation in a memorandum sent back to Washington.

"The entire scene was one of total disorganization and mounting fear, especially since the events taking place in the American Embassy proper were screened from view by buildings and a high wall and no attempt was being made to communicate with the crowd," he said. "Bus movement was beginning to run into increasing difficulty . . . [and] by late afternoon, the bus plan had completely broken down, forcing eight busloads of evacuees to abandon attempts to reach the defense attache office [at Tan Son Nhut Air Base]. These eight busloads eventually sought haven in the [embassy] compound. . . .

"Further evidence of lack of realistic planning was the repeated phone calls from Vietnamese personnel [employed by the U.S. Embassy] who had moved, as per instruction, to 'safe' houses, but were subsequently abandoned. It was also apparent that the American Embassy staff was not prepared for such an evacuation, especially one requiring the helilift of thousands of persons from the American Embassy."

At about 11:00 p.m., there was a lull in helicopter lifts as the final evacuation of the defense attache office began. This caused mounting panic in the embassy compound as rumors circulated that the evacuation was being discontinued. Several Marines held the anchor chain-link fence gate against the pressure from the crowd at the embassy.

"Tension was climbing to the point where people were in danger of being trampled to death by the pressure at the gate," Madison reported. "The situation was clearly beyond the control

of the Marine guards, who began to resort to force. This, in turn, tended to intensify the panic." (One American evacuee suffered a heart attack during the confusion.)

At 1:00 a.m. on Wednesday, April 30, Colonel Harry Summers, Jr., a member of the U.S. delegation to the Four-Party Joint Military Team, and two other Americans moved into the mob in an attempt to calm the fears of the crowd. Colonel Madison tried to do the same with the Marine security guards, who were still worried that the mob would force the gate.

"Once the crowd saw there was some organization within the compound and that the U.S. delegation personnel were willing to share their predicament, the evacuees obeyed orders and organized themselves into two separate columns of family groups," Madison said.

About 30 minutes after midnight, the helicopter lift resumed. It continued through the night, ending at 4:20 a.m. In that time, approximately 3,000 evacuees were helilifted from the American Embassy rooftop and parking lot landing zones.

Left behind were about 420 people, including members of the South Korean Embassy, a German priest who had been working with refugee groups, and Vietnamese employees of the American Embassy and their families. Madison said that he had been assured by U.S. Embassy officials that they would be evacuated but later was told there would be no additional helicopter lifts except those for the remaining U.S. Marines and the delegates to the Four-Party Joint Military Team.

At 4:45 a.m., U.S. Ambassador Graham Martin was evacuated from the embassy. Another group including Madison and Summers departed at 5:24 a.m. Now only a small Marine contingent remained. Now people could only wait.

During this final evacuation, two other American Marines, Captain William C. Nystul, 29, of Coronado, California, and Lieutenant Michael John Shea, 25, of El Paso, Texas, were killed when their helicopter crashed while returning to the carrier *Hancock*. Their deaths added a particularly tragic note to the end of America's 30-year involvement in Vietnam.

Top: *Attacked for the first time since 1973, Saigon suffered under NVA artillery attacks such as the one which decimated this section of the city. The communists now employed large 122mm Russian-made rockets in their attacks.* Far Left: *Americans and South Vietnamese run to board an evacuation helicopter at the defense attache office at Tan Son Nhut Airport.* Left: *Marines rush to take up positions to cover the final evacuation from the embassy.*

195

REFUGEE EVACUATION

"Take it, I've got to fight," the U.S. Marine yelled over the mob as he thrust a tiny Vietnamese boy into the arms of a German clergyman in the U.S. Embassy compound during the final evacuation of Saigon.

Minutes later, with the six-month-old baby cradled in his arms, Pastor Fritz Berhaus was airborne in an American helicopter on his way to one of the ships of the U.S. 7th Fleet in the South China Sea off the coast of South Vietnam, just out of range of North Vietnamese guns.

Berhaus' Peace Village had been caring for 10,000 orphans in the Saigon area. The pastor knew nothing about the boy or what became of his parents.

Such was the chaos during the last days of South Vietnam when entire families were separated.

Waves of American Air Force cargo planes and a U.S. organized sealift began evacuating Vietnamese weeks before the fall of South Vietnam to the North Vietnamese and Viet Cong on April 30, 1975.

Pentagon officials developed an evacuation plan. The familiar Vietnam maps in the Pentagon's National Command Center were marked up with flags and symbols showing ships moving toward the coast with combat-ready Marines, helicopters, fighter-bombers and ammunition. Chartered cargo planes and the Military Airlift Command's C-141 Starlifters and C-5As were also made available.

Officials in Washington kicked around their priorities. Those Vietnamese associated with the U.S. government, such as CIA agents considered "high risk," would have top priority, since they would be in the most danger.

The State Department in Washington hastily set up a task force for the evacuation. On Sunday, April 20, only about 400 people left Vietnam. The next day, 3,000 people, mostly Vietnamese, were evacuated. The U.S. Embassy was still hampered by restrictions on who could leave the country, but officials weren't examining documents too carefully as refugees poured through the gates. The Justice Department announced later it would authorize entry into the United States for tens of thousands of Vietnamese whose lives, it considered, would be in danger if they were left behind. This triggered an even bigger crush to leave the country.

American C-141 jet transports ferried evacuees directly from Saigon to Anderson Air Force Base in Guam, a U.S. territory in the Pacific that was the jumping-off station for refu-

Left: South Vietnamese prepare to disembark from the beach at Vung Tau, fleeing advancing communist troops. At right sits a pile of electric fans which one shopkeeper insisted on bringing with him. Below left: Showing the strain of the flight, a young Vietnamese mother and her children huddle together aboard the USS Blue Ridge. Below right: Assisted by U.S. Marines, South Vietnamese refugees sit in a U.S. landing craft while awaiting transferral to a merchant vessel from the USS Blue Ridge on May 4.

gees en route to the United States. Thousands of refugees were housed in a dusty, hot tent compound in Agana, Guam. Many learned of the fall of Saigon from a local radio station which broadcast three times a day in Vietnamese. The word spread quickly.

The surrender was hardly a surprise. But just the same, many refugees had hoped the city would hold out longer to give loved ones left behind a chance to get out. Now their hopes were dashed.

"I hoped too much," said one man as he picked at a plate of chicken and rice. "Now I cannot hope for anything."

"My brother and brother-in-law are still in Saigon," said a young woman, clutching her four-month-old niece. "I pray that God can help them to come here. Every night we pray."

The American force of more than 40 carriers, amphibious ships, and other vessels were packed with thousands of refugees including high-risk evacuees lifted out of Saigon in the final helicopter evacuation just before the country fell. About 1,000 Americans and 6,000 Vietnamese were evacuated by helicopter during the final U.S. pullout.

U.S. Navy ships picked up about 18,000 refugees who made their way to sea in sampans, rafts and other boats. Some of the ships headed to Subic Bay in the Philippines, and others remained on station to pick up additional refugees.

The air space above the U.S. command ship, the *Blue Ridge*, was jammed with South Vietnamese helicopters waiting to land and drop off evacuees.

Eventually a system was worked out. One helicopter would land on

April 3. A group of Vietnamese orphans sit on the floor of a World Airways DC 8 while refueling at the United States' Yokota Air Base in Tokyo. They are among the first to flee besieged Saigon.

the ship's pad and everybody would jump out. Then the crew would push it overboard, making room for the next one to land. But this took too much time. So helicopters began landing with their engines still running. After all the passengers were out, the pilots took off, swung out to sea and ditched the aircraft, jumping into the water from as high as 100 feet. Navy boats fished the pilots from the water.

South Vietnamese pilots also flew several thousand refugees to Thailand. From there they were flown to Guam aboard U.S. Air Force planes.

Top: *Diving for cover, U.S. Marines dodge flying metal from a South Vietnamese helicopter which crashed on the deck of the USS* Blue Ridge. *Fortunately no one was seriously injured. Confusion and overcrowding resulted in several accidents during the evacuation.* Above: *Vietnamese refugees crowded aboard the Military Sealift Command Ship* Pioneer Contender.

CHAPTER 16
THE SURRENDER

On Wednesday morning, April 30, 1975, United States Marines fired a red smoke grenade to guide a CH-46 helicopter in for a landing on the roof of the American Embassy. Eleven American Marines scrambled aboard and were airborne within four minutes. They had served as the rear guard and were the last Americans to be flown out of Saigon from among 800 Marines who had provided security for the evacuation.

After the American airlift came to an end at 7:52 a.m., hundreds of Vietnamese civilians swarmed into the compound and onto the roof of the embassy. Several hundred Vietnamese huddled together on the roof of a nearby building, hoping for more helicopters.

At the AP bureau, the incoming teletype clicked off a message from Wes Gallagher, AP president, advising that a final helicopter evacuation might be in the works. "Any of you want to leave if it works out?" the message asked.

I replied: "Gallagher: Thanks for your offer. We want to stay, but have some nervous Vietnamese want to get out, please. FYI, U.S. Embassy promised me they would take care of them, but in the chaos they were unable to get into the embassy to board helicopters. Esper."

Just as the U.S. airlift came to an end, North Vietnamese gunners fired a volley of rockets into Tan Son Nhut. A chilling quiet settled over the city as Saigon waited for the North Vietnamese to take over. There would be no more American helicopters.

Two hours later, General Duong Van Minh, who had replaced President Thieu, announced Saigon's unconditional surrender in a radio and television broadcast. General Minh, who had led the coup against Ngo Dinh Diem 12 years earlier, appealed to all Saigon troops to lay down their arms to avoid further bloodshed.

South Vietnamese soldiers carrying heavy backpacks marched from their outposts and garrisons into Saigon to stack their weapons in surrender. They stopped to rest on benches in a park where revelers and lovers had gathered in better days. They were beaten men.

A police officer, a lieutenant colonel, walked to a South Vietnamese war memorial in the park near the National Assembly building. His eyes were filled with sadness; his voice rang out with despair.

Defeated ARVN gather in front of Independence Palace to take instructions from victorious PRG army.

201

Head bowed, the defeated South Vietnamese president, Duong Van Minh, walks out of Independence Palace after surrendering to PRG forces.

202

American-made tanks lie abandoned alongside the road outside Saigon. Their South Vietnamese crews deserted them as the communists advanced on the capital.

North Vietnamese forces parade through the streets of Saigon in their Russian-made T-54 tanks, part of a three-day celebration of the communist victory.

Carrying banners, flags and pictures of Ho Chi Minh, students attend a mass rally outside Independence Palace at which the PRG Military Committee was introduced to the people.

Left: *Still waving the North Vietnamese flag, a Vietnamese youth joins a group of people returning to the town of Cu Chi following the victory celebration in Saigon. Above: May 4. Outside the National Assembly Building on Lam Son Square in Saigon a rally proclaiming the PRG victory draws thousands of Vietnamese.*

Facing page: *Using discarded South Vietnamese Army clothing and a South Vietnamese flag, children stage a mock funeral on a street in Saigon for the GVN.* Above: *Female North Vietnamese cadres form a color guard for a victory parade in Saigon on May 15.* Below: *Saigon VC members destroy a South Vietnamese flag in front of the National Assembly Building in Lam Son Square.*

"Fini! Fini!" he cried.

With that, he saluted the memorial, raised his pistol to his head, and fired. He fell to the ground, mortally wounded.

South Vietnamese soldiers discarded their uniforms and boots on Saigon's streets and changed into civilian clothes to disassociate themselves from the defeated government and the Americans for fear of reprisals.

Within two hours of Saigon's surrender, North Vietnamese and Viet Cong troops rolled into the city on tanks, armored vehicles and camouflaged Chinese-built trucks. Hundreds of South Vietnamese applauded and cheered—perhaps more out of fear than loyalty—as the North Vietnamese columns drove down Unity Boulevard to the Presidential Palace.

The red, blue and yellow starred flag of the National Liberation Front—the southern front organization for North Vietnam—was raised over the Presidential Palace from which Presidents Thieu and Ngo Dinh Diem had directed the war against the communist regime for nearly two decades.

There were small pockets of resistance—the clatter of automatic weapons fire could be heard between the National Assembly building and city hall—but most of the city was quiet.

The North Vietnamese took up positions in a second park facing city hall and huddled against the walls of the shuttered Rex Theater. A Viet Cong flag hung from above the marquee. The Rex was once the headquarters of the joint U.S. Public Affairs Office—JUSPAO—the American propaganda arm that staged the "Five O'Clock Follies," the military briefings that reported victories and body counts of North Vietnamese.

At Tan Son Nhut Air Base, "Pentagon East" lay crumpled, gutted by flames, twisted like a toy command post. The Americans destroyed it themselves with thermite grenades shortly before the evacuation to keep the equipment from falling into North Vietnamese hands.

North Vietnamese took over the U.S. Embassy and Ambassador Graham Martin's residence, sealing them off after they were looted by South Vietnamese. North Vietnamese soldiers took Martin's personal chair as a souvenir. Positions once manned by crew-cut American Marines were now commanded by North Vietnamese guards.

The first night of the North Vietnamese takeover, the chandeliers in the city hall glowed. Flares lighted up the skies. Trucks loaded with North Vietnamese troops and trucks towing artillery moved through Saigon while the city slept. All was quiet. After 30 years of fighting, the city and the country finally belonged to the North Vietnamese and the Viet Cong.

Part of a campaign to eradicate all signs of the former GVN regime, communist supporters destroy a South Vietnamese Ranger Memorial in front of the Saigon Police headquarters with sledgehammers.

208

About the Associated Press

The Associated Press is a nonprofit news-gathering and -distributing association begun in 1848, which now provides more than 10,000 newspapers and radio-television stations in more than 114 countries around the world with news and photographs. Members receive news by teleprinter, by automatic typesetting tape, or directly into computers, and, because the AP is a cooperative organization, they make available to other members the news and pictures collected in their areas. AP's employees are located in 75 foreign offices from Argentina to Zimbabwe and in 128 U.S. cities. Its Saigon bureau was closed by the North Vietnamese in 1975.

About the Author

George Esper has been an Associated Press newsman since 1958. He covered the Indochina War in Vietnam, Cambodia and Laos from 1965 until the fall of South Vietnam in 1975. He served as the Saigon bureau chief from 1973 until five weeks after South Vietnam's fall, when he was expelled by the new communist government. For his coverage of Saigon and its aftermath, Esper received the Associated Press Managing Editors Association's annual top performance award for 1975, and was also cited by the Overseas Press Club. Since then, he has traveled throughout the United States and abroad writing both features and spot news. He makes his home in Massachusetts.